**BASEBALL
SUPERSTARS**

Curt Schilling

✶✶✶✶✶✶✶✶✶✶✶✶✶✶✶✶

Hank Aaron
Ty Cobb
Johnny Damon
Lou Gehrig
Rickey Henderson
Derek Jeter
Randy Johnson
Andruw Jones
Mickey Mantle
Roger Maris

Mike Piazza
Kirby Puckett
Albert Pujols
Mariano Rivera
Jackie Robinson
Babe Ruth
Curt Schilling
Ichiro Suzuki
Bernie Williams
Ted Williams

✶✶✶✶✶✶✶✶✶✶✶✶✶✶✶✶

✷ ✷ ✷ ✷ ✷ ✷ ✷ ✷ ✷ ✷ ✷ ✷ ✷ ✷ ✷

BASEBALL SUPERSTARS

Curt Schilling

Clifford W. Mills

CHELSEA HOUSE
PUBLISHERS
An imprint of Infobase Publishing

✷ ✷ ✷ ✷ ✷ ✷ ✷ ✷ ✷ ✷ ✷ ✷ ✷ ✷ ✷

Chelsea House
An imprint of Infobase Publishing
132 West 31st Street
New York NY 10001

Library of Congress Cataloging-in-Publication Data
Mills, Cliff, 1947-
  Curt Schilling / Clifford W. Mills.
      p. cm. — (Baseball superstars)
  Includes bibliographical references and index.
  ISBN 978-0-7910-9635-2 (hardcover)
  1. Schilling, Curt. 2. Baseball players—United States—Biography. I. Title. II. Series.
  GV865.S33M55 2008
  796.357092—dc22
  [B]   2007028939

Series design by Erik Lindstrom
Cover design by Ben Peterson and Jooyoung An

Printed in the United States of America

Bang EJB 10 9 8 7 6 5 4 3 2 1

This book is printed on acid-free paper.

CONTENTS

A Night to Remember

Some of the 56,000 baseball fans who were huddled in Yankee Stadium on the night of Tuesday, October 19, 2004, say that the second thing they remember about the evening was how the cold air roamed around the legendary old park. The chill seemed to probe for weaknesses and exposed skin. The near-freezing breezes were merciless. No one could get comfortable.

The first thing many remember is the red stain of blood on the white sock worn by a Boston Red Sox pitcher named Curt Schilling. Schilling was not supposed to pitch in this crucial sixth game of the American League Championship Series between the New York Yankees and the Red Sox. He had a partly torn and dislocated tendon in his right ankle—the ankle that right-handed pitchers use to push off the mound. It is an injury familiar to skiers who fall backward and do not release from their bindings. It is a similar injury to one that hits some three-year-old thoroughbred racehorses, forcing them to be removed from the track permanently.

That night, Yankee Stadium turned into a giant theater, as it sometimes does in October when the Yankees are playing. The drama had several acts. Each time Schilling pushed off the mound, he did not know if that would be his last pitch. He had to fight to keep his balance after he threw. He was facing one of the most powerful lineups of hitters in baseball history, the New York Yankees. They had been world champions four out of the previous eight seasons. The Red Sox had not won a world championship since 1918, and many fans felt that the team had been "cursed" when they traded Babe Ruth to the Yankees after the 1919 season. "The Curse of the Bambino" was very real for many fans, and Yankee supporters did their best to keep it alive. The Yankees had beaten the Red Sox so many times in crucial games during the past few years that Red Sox fans had almost given up. Curt Schilling had been signed to help break the curse. He promised he would. Many feel that on that chilly night he did.

Schilling had injured his ankle several days before in the first game of the American League Division Series against the Anaheim Angels. He had tried to field a ground ball and twisted his ankle sharply as he came off the pitcher's mound. He dislocated a tendon. Schilling was determined to pitch in the first game of the American League Championship Series against the Yankees, but his performance was so bad that he was removed after giving up six runs in only three innings. Schilling later told reporters, "I couldn't push off. I thought if I could make pitches, I could keep us in the game, but I couldn't. It affected both my command and velocity." Pitchers have two main weapons: speed and location. The injured Schilling had no weapons.

Curt Schilling tended to his right ankle during the third inning of Game 6 of the 2004 American League Championship Series against the New York Yankees. The Red Sox team physician had operated on Schilling's torn tendon hours before the game, and his ankle started to bleed when a suture pulled out.

The Red Sox became demoralized after their star pitcher was beaten so badly by the Yankees, and they lost the next two games as well. They even gave up 19 runs to the Yankees in Game 3. No team in baseball history had ever come back after losing the first three games of a series, and the Red Sox were being called "pathetic." Some players, wearing "Why Not

Us?" T-shirts, were hanging their heads and unable to speak to reporters after the embarrassing Game 3. The team had not won a World Series in 86 years, and this year now seemed as if it would be no different from the previous ones.

FRANKENSTEIN'S PITCHER

Somehow the Red Sox came back and won Games 4 and 5 in their home, Fenway Park, but the team was still not expected to win a Game 6 or 7 in Yankee Stadium. The pitchers were dead-tired, and Schilling was considered injured, probably unable to pitch again for many months. Team doctor William Morgan searched for cases in which an ankle injury like Schilling's had been treated successfully with a short recovery time. He found none. He had already tried ankle braces and modified cleats, and they did not work. So, he then did something extraordinary. He came up with an entirely new medical procedure. Morgan reasoned that he could sew the injured tendon back in place, both helping with its tear and keeping it from sliding out of its natural groove and rubbing painfully against the ankle bones. Since there were no existing operations to follow, he first tried out the procedure on a cadaver (a dead body donated by a medical school).

When reporters found out about the experiment, they began to write about Dr. Frankenstein scavenging graveyards for body parts. Curt Schilling, they joked, was about to become "Frankenstein's pitcher." Rumors started that the doctor was going to place the healthy tendon of a dead man into Schilling's lower leg. The rumors were not true, but that did not stop them.

Six hours before the start of Game 6, Morgan asked Schilling to lie on a training table, and Morgan began to stitch the skin around the dislocated ankle tendon to the tissue close to the bone. He gave Schilling a painkiller. When asked later if the procedure had hurt, Schilling replied, "What do you think? Does it hurt when you get poked in the eye?" When Red Sox general manager Theo Epstein was asked about the procedure, he replied, "There were a lot of scenarios we looked at, and one scenario was a last-ditch scenario with sutures." When Schilling was asked later about the operation, he said, "This was an absolutely last-gasp, brilliant idea. Because, had this not worked, I would not have been able to pitch Game 6. No way." Modern medicine had saved the day, or at least delayed defeat for another day.

THE BLOODY SOCK

The Red Sox not only needed Schilling to pitch in Game 6, they also needed him to pitch at least six innings. He was the only pitcher other than the relievers who had a rested arm. On that Tuesday, he began his warm-ups at exactly 6:45 P.M., as he always did before a night game. He tested his ankle and did not flinch as he threw his first warm-ups. Soon, it was time.

The game began in the frigid night air. The Red Sox batted but did not score. Schilling walked out of the Red Sox dugout and kissed a necklace he always wears when he pitches. Like many baseball players, Schilling has several rituals he performs before a game. Kissing the necklace is the most obvious one. He also never steps on the foul line when walking to and from the pitcher's mound. He crossed the third-base line and reached the mound. He watched the Yankee hitter Derek Jeter dig into the batter's box and waggle his bat. Schilling finally threw his first pitch. Dr. Morgan held his breath.

Schilling pitched brilliantly at first. Then, some fans and the announcers in the Fox-TV booth noticed something on Schilling's right white sock, the one worn under a player's regular stirrup socks. What they saw was bright red blood from a wound created when one of the stitches pulled out. One fan reportedly yelled, "It's Roy Hobbs!" Hobbs was the fictional character in the book and movie *The Natural* whose injuries caused him to bleed into his uniform during the biggest game of his life. Red Sox Nation watched and could hardly breathe.

In the fourth inning, the Red Sox scored four runs when Jason Varitek singled in a run and Mark Bellhorn hit a three-run homer. Schilling gave up a home run to Yankee slugger Bernie Williams, but at the end of seven innings, the Red Sox were ahead 4-1 and Schilling had worked as long as he could. He was bleeding and exhausted. He had saved the Red Sox season and kept their hopes alive.

THE SLAP

In the eighth inning, Red Sox pitcher Bronson Arroyo came in and immediately got into trouble. The Yankees scored once and were about to rally when "The Slap" became part of the legendary story of the sixth game. Yankee Alex Rodriguez hit a ground ball to Arroyo, who ran to tag "A-Rod." Rodriguez slapped Arroyo's arm, knocking the ball out of his glove, and Rodriguez went on to second base as the ball rolled away. Derek Jeter scored, and the Yankees were on their way to one of their famous eighth-inning comebacks against the Sox. Boston fans groaned and knew the curse was still alive.

Then, something strange happened. The umpires met and ruled that Rodriguez had interfered with the pitcher, and he was out. Jeter had to come back to first base, and his run was erased. The rally was killed. The Yankee fans threw so many objects onto the field in protest that the game had to be stopped as Red Sox manager Terry Francona pulled his players into their dugout for safety. Riot police had to be brought out—the first time in major-league history that riot police had been called onto the field for at least a full inning. All the force of the historic Red Sox-Yankee conflicts came howling into Yankee Stadium with the cold wind. The theater had turned into a madhouse.

When order was restored, the game began again. Finally, Tony Clark struck out in the ninth inning against reliever Keith Foulke, and the Red Sox won, 4-2. The series was now even,

Curt Schilling's bloody sock was far from the only drama in that famous Game 6. Here, the Yankees' Alex Rodriguez swats at the arm of Red Sox pitcher Bronson Arroyo, who was trying to tag Rodriguez out in the eighth inning. The umpires determined that Rodriguez had interfered with Arroyo, nullifying a Yankee run. The New York fans threw objects onto the field in protest, and riot police were needed to restore the calm.

and the Red Sox became the first team in baseball history to tie up a series after falling behind three games to none. Game 6 became a legendary night.

"THE GREATEST BASEBALL STORY EVER TOLD"

A flood of online, radio, television, and newspaper stories immediately washed over the baseball world concerning Game 6. When asked about the game later, Schilling said, "When you care about your teammates enough, you do things you never thought you could do." Tim McCarver, one of the Fox announcers, said, "Curt Schilling's performance tonight will long live in New England baseball lore." The Red Sox pitching coach, Dave Wallace, said, "What he did put him with [St. Louis Cardinal hero Bob] Gibson, [Dodger great Sandy] Koufax, and those guys." A Red Sox Web site called the Boston Dirt Dogs posted a message: "For one big

★ ★ ★ ★ ★ ★

THE FASTBALL

The basic pitch is the fastball, thrown at every level of baseball. It gets to home plate faster than any other pitch, giving the batter less time to make a decision about what to do. It can intimidate and overpower.

The fastball comes in several varieties. The most common is the four-seam fastball, so called because the fingers touch the seams in four places. The pitcher finds the horseshoe part of the ball where the seams are farthest apart, puts his index and middle fingers perpendicular to the seams at that part of the ball, and places his thumb on the opposite side of the ball, so it does not touch any seams. The four-seamer is the most reliable pitch because of what a batter sees. The batter is watching the ball come at him or her, and the spin of the ball is hard to pick up— there is no "flicker" of red from the spinning seams because the ball is spinning in such a way that more seams are seen in every rotation, so much so that the seams blur together.

night, Curt Schilling was Larry Bird, Tom Brady, Bobby Orr, and Ted Williams all rolled into one." *New York Times* writer Dave Anderson wrote that "whenever people think about Schilling in the years to come, that's the scene they will remember—the smudge of blood on his white sock as much as the downward disappearance of his splitter [a kind of fastball that is thrown with the fingers far apart] for seven sturdy innings." The bloody sock was taken immediately to the Baseball Hall of Fame in Cooperstown, New York. Schilling said later that he wanted to nominate Dr. Morgan for the Nobel Prize in medicine. He may have been only half-kidding.

☆ ☆ ☆ ☆ ☆ ☆

With a two-seam fastball, the pitcher grips the ball where the seams are closest together, and places his index and middle finger parallel to the laces. The ball shows fewer laces per spin, so it "flickers." The batter can get a better idea of whether the ball has topspin, and therefore is a curveball, or has backspin and is a fastball. Knowing the difference helps the batter make a decision about when and where to swing.

The four-seamer tends to be straighter than a two-seamer. To put more movement on the fastball, the pitcher may throw a "cutter" (holding the two-seamer off-center) or a "splitter" (putting the index and middle finger on different sides of the ball). The splitter is really a slower fastball called a fast changeup, because the ball slips more than if the fingers were pushing with maximum force. It comes to home plate about 5 to 10 miles per hour (8 to 16 kilometers per hour) slower than a regular fastball. The batter thinks it is a fastball and is ahead of the pitch.

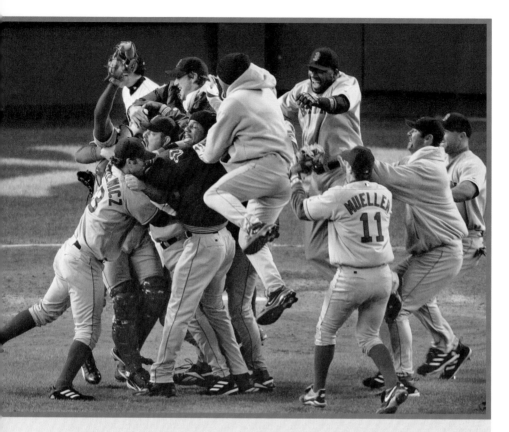

Players from the Red Sox celebrated their win over the New York Yankees to capture the American League pennant in 2004. The Sox are the only team to win a seven-game series after falling behind three games to none. Boston went on to sweep St. Louis in the World Series to finally break the "Curse of the Bambino."

The Red Sox took inspiration from Game 6. Before Game 7 the next night, many of them watched the movie *Miracle*, about the 1980 men's gold-medal Olympic hockey team. Johnny Damon and Kevin Millar, two players who had called themselves and their teammates "idiots," gave emotional speeches in a cramped locker room. They talked about how much they had been through together as a team. Millar said, "This is where heroes are made." He was right. The Red Sox won, 10-3, with big home runs coming from Damon and David Ortiz. Derek Lowe pitched well for the Red Sox, and at 12:01 A.M. on Thursday, October 21, the final Yankee was put out. The Red Sox had made history—they had beaten the Yankees.

The Curse of the Bambino, however, was not yet reversed. The Red Sox had to win the World Series, not just the American League pennant. Only when the Red Sox went on to sweep the 2004 World Series from the St. Louis Cardinals did the largest celebration in the 374-year history of Boston begin. Reporter Dan Shaughnessy wrote for the *Boston Globe*:

> They did it for the old folks in Presque Isle, Maine, and White River Junction, Vt. They did it for the baby boomers in North Conway, N.H., and Groton, Mass. They did it for the kids in Central Falls, R.I., and Putnam, Conn. While church bells rang in small New England towns and horns honked on the crowded streets of the Hub, the 2004 Red Sox last night won the 100th World Series. . . . No more Curse of the Bambino. No more taunts of "1918."

The Red Sox won the final game under a lunar eclipse, on the same date of their Game 7 loss in the famous 1986 World Series. ESPN analyst Tim Kurkjian said of the 2004 Sox world championship, "This is the greatest baseball story ever told." No Red Sox fan would ever disagree.

Sports Illustrated named the entire team "Sportsmen of the Year." Because Schilling had also been named co-Sportsman of the Year in 2001 with teammate Randy Johnson, he became only the second athlete ever to win the award twice. Tiger Woods is the other. Schilling became famous the world over, as did his bloody sock. He had come a very long way from his hometown of Anchorage, Alaska. That is where his story begins.

Growing Up North and South

Anchorage, Alaska, is not the birthplace of many professional athletes. It is, however, Alaska's largest city and the port through which most of the goods and people coming to Alaska must pass. In the winter months, residents have to go to work and come home from work in the dark, since the city is located at such a high latitude. The few days of summer are usually mild but often filled with rain and mosquitoes. There are few worse places to play baseball in the United States.

There were two bases in Anchorage on which military men and women served—Elmendorf Air Force Base and Fort Richardson. The military was a major employer in Anchorage, especially in the days before oil was found in Prudhoe Bay, to the north. One of the largest earthquakes ever to hit an American city, a 9.2 on the Richter scale, rumbled into

Anchorage in March 1964, and the military continued to help with the cleanup for many months after the quake.

On November 14, 1966, the boxer Muhammad Ali reached the peak of his career and defeated Cleveland "Big Cat" Williams in the third round of a much anticipated match. On that day, fighting in a faraway country named Vietnam was intensifying, and a man named Ronald Reagan had just been elected governor of the state of California. On that same day, a son was born to a couple in Anchorage named Cliff and Mary Schilling, and they named him Curtis Montague Schilling. He was their second child and their first boy.

A FAMILY ON THE MOVE

Cliff and Mary Schilling had moved to Anchorage as part of Cliff's military duties. Cliff was an athletic and disciplined man who had always loved baseball. He knew that, if he ever had a son, the crib would have to have a baseball glove and baseball in it. Of course, the new baby soon found both next to him. Being born near the beginning of winter meant that the baby would not be spending a great deal of his first few months outdoors. The ball and glove would be among the first things he saw and felt.

Like many military families, the Schillings moved often and moved great distances. Making new friends so many times is always difficult for children, but "army brats" are famous for becoming outgoing and adjusting quickly to changing houses and schools. The Schillings moved many places, but eventually settled near Scottsdale, Arizona, in a town called Paradise Valley. They were near Phoenix, very much the opposite of Anchorage, Alaska, in terms of playing baseball. The Phoenix area is one of the warmest large-urban areas in the world, with only some Persian Gulf cities being warmer.

Curt played baseball wherever he was as a child, but in Paradise Valley he could play all year round. His father knew that Curt had a gift by the time the boy was eight years old. He could throw a baseball very far and very hard. When fathers play catch with their sons, they often praise their growing players. Cliff, though, was not given to playful talk and easy exaggerations. He simply told his son that his throwing arm would "let you be what you want to be." It was up to Curt to decide who he wanted to be.

ORGANIZED BALL

Arizona in the 1970s and 1980s had many youth leagues that a baseball player could join. Curt played every chance he could. He was not a pitcher at first. He played third base, a position that demanded the strongest arm in the infield. Young men who can throw across the diamond and hit a small target at first base are unusual. Third base is called "the hot corner" because of the speed at which balls fly off the bat and get to the fielder. The first baseman usually plays farther back from home plate than the third baseman does, so the most fearless baseball player on the field is often playing third. That player must "guard the line" as well, making sure that few balls pass over or near third base and travel down the right side of the foul line for extra-base hits.

As a teenager, Curt attended Shadow Mountain High School, part of the Paradise Valley Unified School District. The school had only opened in 1974, so Curt had the advantage of attending a relatively large and new school with excellent athletic facilities and a good baseball field. Shadow Mountain would become well known for its athletes. Besides Schilling, Sacramento Kings point guard Mike Bibby is a Shadow Mountain graduate, as is Olympic gold-medal-winning swimmer Misty Hyman and Detroit Lions wide receiver Shaun McDonald. Curt would not have to struggle to find excellent coaching and a high level of competition. He made the baseball team as its third baseman. When his coach noticed that Curt had a strong and accurate arm, he asked Curt to do a little pitching.

TRYING OUT FOR THE CINCINNATI REDS

The professional baseball organization of the Cincinnati Reds was thorough and efficient throughout the 1960s, 1970s, and 1980s. The Reds were a big red scouting machine. But the Reds also had tryout camps around the country for players who might have been overlooked by their professional scouts. The Reds held a tryout camp near Phoenix when Curt was in his junior year at Shadow Mountain. He found out about it and decided to attend.

The tryout camps are usually for high school seniors, graduates, and even college players. Curt, though, did not lack confidence in himself, even at this early stage. He figured he had nothing to lose. When he arrived at the camp, he was given a number and told to attach it to the back of his jersey. He was then told to line up to participate in a 40-yard-dash drill with several other players, to see how fast a runner he was. Curt had to think quickly. He knew he was not a fast runner, and he knew he would not have a second chance to make a first impression on the scouts watching him. He also knew that pitchers did not have to take part in the 40-yard-dash drill, because scouts never care how fast a pitcher can run. They only care how fast he can throw a baseball. So, Curt decided to line up with the pitchers, since he had done a little throwing at Shadow Mountain.

Each tryout pitcher was sent to the mound and told to throw some pitches after warming up. A scout stood behind the pitcher to call out his number to others. Another scout stood behind a backstop with a radar gun, measuring how fast a player threw a pitch. The average high school pitcher throws 70 to 75 miles per hour (113 to 121 kilometers per hour). The average college pitcher throws 80 to 85 miles per hour (129 to 137 kilometers per hour).

Curt finally got his chance to take the mound. No one had ever timed one of his pitches before, so he had no idea what to expect. He took a deep breath, went into his windup, and threw the ball to home plate with all of his might. The sound of the ball hitting the catcher's glove could be heard far into the outfield. Heads turned. The catcher returned the ball to Curt, and he did it again. After several pitches, Curt walked off the mound, and a scout came over to him and asked him to repeat his name. The scout said, "You hit 90 miles per hour [145 kilometers per hour] on the gun." From that moment on, Curt knew that he was a pitcher and that he wanted to play for a major-league team.

The scout was disappointed to find out that Curt was only 17 years old and a junior in high school. According to baseball rules, Curt could not be signed to a contract until he was 18. The scout told him to keep pitching and said the Reds would keep track of him.

BECOMING A THINKING MAN

Curt threw himself into pitching during his senior year in high school. The Shadow Mountain Matadors had a good pitching staff already, and as a new pitcher Curt was not able to get as many chances to pitch as he would have liked. When he did pitch, though, he performed well.

Curt was smart and a good student, especially in subjects he had an interest in. His favorite subject was history, and he developed a strong attraction to the subject during this time. He would later become a serious student of military history, especially the events and people of World War II. He soon developed another interest. In the early 1980s, personal computers became popular, and Curt was like many other young men and women—he fell in love with his first Apple computer. The Apple II was very popular in the late 1970s and early 1980s, and sales were pushed because it could run a spreadsheet program called VisiCalc. The program could keep track of rows

The Apple II computer, one of the first personal computers, was popular in the late 1970s and early 1980s. As a high school student, Curt Schilling had an Apple II and became proficient in using its spreadsheet programs and playing computer games on it. Even today, Schilling remains a computer "geek."

and columns of numbers and calculate changes instantly, something that had taken accountants hours and days to do for as long as anyone could remember. Curt's active mind was made for computing and video games. Soon, he would be playing "Wizardry," an Apple II sword and sorcery game. He became a lifelong computer "geek."

Curt knew by now that he had talent, and he wanted to become a professional pitcher. He had a choice to make when he graduated from Shadow Mountain. He could wait to get drafted by a professional team, or he could go to college, play baseball, and develop himself in many ways. He was not an experienced pitcher, and he knew he had a lot to learn. So, he chose to go to college. He liked Arizona and did not want to be too far from his family. So in September 1985, he enrolled in Yavapai Junior College (now Yavapai College) in Prescott, Arizona. Prescott is a small city in central Arizona, more than a mile above sea level and therefore, more moderate in temperature than the Phoenix area. It had started as a mining town when gold was discovered nearby in 1863, and it has the look and feel of a Midwestern town more than almost any other place in the American Southwest. Prescott is a wonderful place to attend college.

BEING DRAFTED

Yavapai had a very successful baseball program, and coach David Dangler would probably have known about Schilling from the Reds' tryout camp. He might also have known about Schilling's ability from the summer league that Schilling had played in. Dangler's teams were well coached, and they played in the Arizona Community College Athletic Conference (ACCAC), a very competitive league. Scouts often came to ACCAC games and to the summer-league games played in Arizona.

One scout roaming through the ACCAC and the Southwest territory was Ray Boone. Boone had been a good major-league third baseman for many teams and had retired from the Boston Red Sox in 1960 to become one of their scouts. His son Bob would become one of the best defensive catchers in baseball history, and Bob's sons Bret and Aaron would also become All-Stars. (They are the only family to have three generations of All-Stars. As a Yankee, Aaron Boone would ruin the 2003 Red Sox season with a walk-off home run in the famous Game 7 of the American League Championship Series.) Ray Boone saw that Schilling had a special combination of qualities that were rare in a young pitcher—he was big (now 6 feet 4 inches and more than 200 pounds—193 centimeters and more than 90 kilograms), he did not seem to tire in a game after throwing

Detroit Tigers infielder Ray Boone relaxed with his sons, Rodney *(left)* and Bob, in the dugout during spring training in 1954. Boone later played briefly for the Boston Red Sox and became a scout for the team after he retired from playing. Boone took a liking to a young Curt Schilling and persuaded the Red Sox to select him in the January 1986 draft.

many hard pitches, he was confident, and he was tough. When he did not do well, he seemed to forget about it quickly.

Until 1987, baseball had two amateur drafts each year—one in January and one in June (only the one in June is held now). Ray Boone convinced the Red Sox that they should draft Schilling. He wanted to beat other teams, especially the Reds, to this unproven but talented player. Boone agreed that the team did not have to offer Schilling a contract until he proved himself at Yavapai—they could "draft and follow," which meant they had a year from drafting him to sign him to a contract.

So, in January 1986, Schilling waited by the phone on draft day to see what would happen. He received a call in the afternoon of January 14 and was told that the Red Sox had drafted him in the second round. He was thrilled. The team always needed pitchers, and he thought he would have a better chance

☆ ☆ ☆ ☆ ☆ ☆

THE JUNIOR COLLEGE WORLD SERIES

Every year the best college baseball teams in the United States take part in two different college world series. One is in Omaha, Nebraska, for teams from larger four-year universities. The other is in Grand Junction, Colorado, for teams from smaller colleges, often two-year institutions. This world series is called the "JUCO World Series" or just "JUCO," for its junior-college origins. In 2007, some 127,000 fans celebrated the fiftieth anniversary of JUCO at Suplizio Field, named after one of the founders of the series. On June 2, a national audience watched on the College Sports Television network as Chipola College (from Florida) defeated mighty New Mexico Junior College. Chipola scored 34 runs on 46 hits in the final two days to win its first world series.

Several well-known major-league players have played in JUCO, including Curt Schilling; reliever Eric Gagné; pitcher David Wells, who threw a perfect game in 1998; and batting champion Kirby Puckett. Some teams have had as many as 14 major-league draftees on them, as a recent San Jacinto (Texas) College-North team did. San Jacinto is the New York Yankees of the JUCO, appearing in the world series 16 times.

of becoming a major leaguer with them than with anyone else. His fate would be tied to the Red Sox.

PLAYING IN COLLEGE: HIS FIRST WORLD SERIES

Schilling learned a lesson very early during his winter training with the Yavapai team. In high school, all he had to do was throw the ball into the middle of the strike zone as fast as he could, and very few players could hit it. He would simply

☆ ☆ ☆ ☆ ☆

The series' opening-night banquet is famous, and guest speakers have included Yankee owner George Steinbrenner, Hall of Famers Willie Mays and Paul Molitor, and Yankee manager Joe Torre. Some speakers recall the early days, when a few people organized the tournament from their basement. The first JUCO winner in Grand Junction was a 10-player team from Paris, Texas—legend has it that the players piled into two cars and drove all night to get to Colorado for the series.

The weeklong JUCO World Series is big business for the city of Grand Junction, Colorado, and it is western Colorado's premier sporting event. Grand Junction is named for the intersection of the Colorado and Gunnison rivers, just east of the Utah state line. It has had a boom-and-bust history, growing rich on silver in the 1880s and oil shale in the 1970s and becoming devastated when those resources were depleted or lost value. Several Grand Junction citizens had the foresight to bring JUCO to the city in 1959. The series made a profit of $43 that year. In 2007, the tourism dollars are significantly more than that.

overpower the opposition. In college, the players were different. Their reaction times were better, and they were stronger. Their bats moved through the strike zone faster and with more power. They could hit almost any ball thrown straight down the middle of home plate, no matter how hard it was thrown. All of a sudden, Schilling was hit, and hit hard.

Baseball instructors say that players start as throwers and then become pitchers only when they learn to fool the batter. The pitcher must control where the ball is thrown, vary the speed of the pitch, and make it break in some way so the batter does not know where to swing the bat each time. And it all starts with the windup.

Coach Dangler saw that he had to work on Schilling's windup, which was not the same each time. The best pitchers use exactly the same motion as they prepare to throw the ball. They are consistent, and they are balanced. Dangler helped Schilling to be both. For a young player, the right coaching at the right time makes all the difference, but the player must be able to accept the advice. He has to be willing to learn and practice what he has been told.

Schilling's first game at Yavapai was against Pima Community College in the early spring of 1986. Pima was a good team, and its players hit Schilling hard at first. He gave up four runs but settled down and got better as the game continued. He put into practice what he had learned. He mixed his pitches so that the batters did not know what to expect; soon he was able to throw the ball where he wanted and make hitting it most difficult. His team won, 6-4.

Dangler soon realized how valuable Schilling was to his team. He used Schilling both as a starting pitcher and as a reliever. Many young pitchers are one or the other. The relief pitcher has to be able to warm up quickly and have the toughness to face batters in difficult situations when the game can be won or lost. Schilling had that toughness. He liked the challenge of having the game won or lost on his efforts.

College hitters use aluminum bats. Professional players use wooden bats. The difference is greater than most people think, with aluminum bats giving hitters a big advantage. Scouts realize that and know that some pitchers will get hit harder in college than they will in the major leagues. They knew that Schilling would be more successful when pitching inside against hitters using wooden bats—those bats would break, not result in hits.

Schilling won 10 games with Yavapai and only lost two. The team won its division with a record of 17–9 (Schilling got more than half of the wins, so he must have been pitching a great deal). The team was invited to the Junior College World Series in 1986 and finished third in the nation. Schilling was a big part of Yavapai's success. He had his first taste of being in a very big game. It would not be his last. He had proven something to himself and to others. He was ready for the next step.

Getting
to the Bigs

The Red Sox, and other teams, were impressed with what they saw of Curt Schilling's pitching at Yavapai and in the Junior College World Series. He had given up more runs than they would have liked, but he had not been afraid of hitters and had not lost his composure when he was hit hard. He was always improving, always trying to get better. So many players become satisfied with their level of play that professional teams are on the lookout for someone with the need to continuously improve. In Schilling, they found that.

On May 30, 1986, Schilling signed his first major-league contract—with the Boston Red Sox. Ray Boone's insight had paid off. Schilling was now a professional player, and he was headed for the opposite part of the country. He said goodbye to his family and friends and headed to Elmira, New York, the home of a Red Sox minor-league team in the New York-Penn League, an "A" league. The minor leagues have Rookie-level and Class A, AA, and AAA teams. The players at the Rookie and Class A levels are the most inexperienced and farthest from getting to the major leagues, while the players in AAA are the best and closest to getting the call to the majors. Schilling was starting at the bottom.

DOING TIME IN ELMIRA

Still a teenager, Schilling found living on his own in Elmira to be quite a different experience from being in his parents' house. He was free to do what he wanted when he wanted and, like many young people, he did not handle so much freedom as well as he might have. He tended to give parties, stay up late, and not concentrate on his off days as much as a coach could have wanted.

On the days he pitched, however, Schilling was all business. He adjusted quickly to the new hitters, who were much better than he was used to, but he raised the level of his pitching. He would later say, "The guys I played with in rookie ball, the worst players, were 100 times better than anybody I ever played with in high school." Even most college players are no match for most professional pitching.

He was helped now that only wooden bats were being used against him. Bloop hits from aluminum bats were becoming easy fly outs to the infield from shattered wooden bats. He could now pitch the ball on the inside part of home plate (and even inside into the batter's box) and not give up many hits. He could make the batters uncomfortable, especially if they thought a 90-mile-per-hour (145-kilometer-per-hour) fastball was headed at them. Schilling loved the confrontations with professional batters.

He was still a relatively inexperienced pitcher, however, and needed more coaching to show him how to approach each batter with a plan. The Red Sox were unusual—they did not have full-time pitching coaches for their minor-league teams. Former pitcher Lee Stange would travel from team to team, and he came to Elmira a few times to meet with the pitchers. Stange had been a successful relief pitcher for several teams, including the famous 1967 "Impossible Dream" Red Sox (who lost the World Series to the St. Louis Cardinals). Pitching coaches were not paid as well then as they are now, and the science of teaching pitchers was not as well developed. For a young pitcher, the Red Sox may not have been the best place to start, since they did not have a track record of developing young pitchers

★ ★ ★ ★ ★ ★
BATS: WOOD AND ALUMINUM COMPETE

Every pitcher's nightmare is being hit in the face with a batted ball. Studies show that pitchers need .375 seconds on average to react to a ball coming at them. Only about 5 percent of balls hit by wooden bats travel that fast, but more than half of the balls hit by aluminum bats in the hands of college players do.

Aluminum bats became popular in the 1970s and 1980s for many reasons. The most obvious one is that they do not break, so teams and schools save money. The bats also allow the hitter to hit the ball farther. The aluminum bat has a hollow core, and because of that it acts like a trampoline when a ball hits it—it flexes and does not compress the baseball as much as a wooden bat does when the ball is hit. A ball that compresses less has more energy and flies off the bat faster. The faster a ball is going when it leaves the bat, the farther it will travel. And the quicker it will get back to the pitcher's mound.

in their farm system. Schilling called Lee Stange "The Stinger" but never felt he got much coaching from him or anyone else. Nonetheless, Schilling did well in his first year at Elmira, finishing with a record of 7–3. His earned run average (the average number of runs he allowed every nine innings—called an ERA) was 2.59. Any ERA under 3.00 was good.

The 1986 Red Sox are a famous team, and as a minor leaguer within the organization, Schilling found one major leaguer whom he especially looked up to and wanted to be like. Roger Clemens had a record of 24–4 in 1986 and led the Red Sox to the World Series. He was only four years older than

★ ★ ★ ★ ★ ★

The other reason players can hit a ball farther with an aluminum bat is that it has a balance point closer to the batter's hands. The center of the mass in a bat is crucial. The bat is a lever, and levers have balance points, like seesaws. The closer the balance point is to the hands of a batter, the faster the bat can be swung (more of the lever is used to hit the ball). The faster the bat, the greater the exit speed of the ball. The faster the exit speed, the greater the distance it will travel.

High schools, colleges, and bat manufacturers have been negotiating about how to limit the "hotness" of an aluminum bat. Standards are often changing, but for many years the maximum exit speed of a batted ball was supposed to be 97 miles per hour (156 kilometers per hour). That exit speed gives pitchers enough time to react to a ball hit back at them, at least in theory. In practice, some pitchers still get hit, and a few have even died. Some say that, if aluminum bats were allowed in the major leagues, a pitcher might be killed each and every year.

Schilling and was the same kind of pitcher—big, strong, and hard-throwing. Schilling hoped to be the same kind of power pitcher. He watched Clemens carefully. He, too, wanted to strike out as many batters as he could. Striking out a batter was the pitcher's ultimate victory. The idea of valuing wins more than strikeouts was not widely accepted then, and Schilling dreamed of being a strikeout artist. Schilling was ready to challenge better hitters. He was promoted to the next level.

HEADING SOUTH

In 1987, Schilling was now ready to go to the best Red Sox Class A club, the Greensboro, North Carolina, team in the South Atlantic League (also called the "Sally" League). Greensboro was yet another change of culture for Schilling. It was not like Anchorage, or Arizona, or New York. Greensboro had been famous for the civil-rights demonstrations started at a Woolworth's lunch counter when four black students were denied service in 1960. Members of the Communist Workers Party and the Ku Klux Klan had clashed there in 1979, resulting in the deaths of five Communist Workers Party members. For the first time in his life, Schilling was seeing and experiencing Southern culture and history.

He did not adjust well, for whatever reason. The team was not as good as some of its competition. Schilling still did not have a pitching coach. Left on his own, he tried to be like Roger Clemens. He wanted to strike everyone out. He did lead the Sally League in strikeouts, with 189 for the year, but he lost almost twice as many games as he won—8 wins and 15 losses.

Schilling wanted to know what he was doing wrong and what he was doing right. He asked other pitchers for advice. He listened to what they were saying and watched what they were doing. Even at his most discouraged point, he was still determined to become a major leaguer. The 1987 season, however, was his worst year in professional baseball, and his life was about to get much worse on the most personal level.

LOSING A FATHER

Cliff Schilling had been forced to retire from the military because of heart troubles. He had been a soldier for 22 years and served his country well. He had moved to Colorado and taken a job in law enforcement but was diagnosed with a brain tumor. He decided to visit Curt in Arizona in January 1988, before he became too sick to travel.

The father and son had been close but had not spent a great deal of time talking to each other about their lives and their feelings. Like many fathers and sons, they found it hard to open up. That changed the week Cliff visited his son. On their last night together, Schilling later said, "We stayed up late that night just talking about baseball, life, everything. He said things that a father usually thinks but doesn't say. I remember him saying how he knew I was going to make it to the big leagues."

The next morning, they were ready to leave the house for the airport when Cliff collapsed. Schilling called 911 and held his father in his arms. Cliff was suffering from an aortic aneurysm, a swelling of the major artery connected to the heart. The aneurysm can burst, and it is usually fatal when it does. The paramedics arrived, only to find Cliff dead in his son's arms. They could do nothing to bring him back to life.

Schilling had to tell his mother that Cliff had died. They were both devastated. His father had been a strong presence all his life, and now that presence was gone. "My father was the glue that held us together. When he died, I kind of lost my family." He is still not close to his older sister or his mother. His life had reached a low point, and he began to rebel against the losses he felt.

LOSING ONE TEAM AND GAINING ANOTHER

The New Britain Red Sox were a good AA team in 1988. They played at Beehive Field in New Britain, Connecticut. The city, southwest of Hartford, has been known as "The Hardware City" for as long as anyone can remember—Stanley Tools has its headquarters there. The baseball field was known as a pitcher's park—center field was nearly 500 feet (152 meters) from home plate, and baseballs came to die there instead of fly out of the park for home runs.

Schilling reported for duty in New Britain at the start of the 1988 season, even though he was still reeling from the loss of his father. He was in pain, and acted up and partied. Some people in the Red Sox front office began to wonder if he was serious enough to apply himself at this new level. He had his "army brat" brashness to get him through anything, and even though his coaches may have felt he was loud and not serious enough, he was still serious enough to survive. The batters in this AA league were the best he had ever faced, and he still had to coach himself. Schilling, though, did well enough to have an 8–5 record by the middle of the 1988 season. He was not striking out nearly as many batters as he had in the past, but he was winning more of his games. The big field helped him.

One day in July 1988, Schilling was talking to some teammates about the rumors that Brady Anderson, an outfielder with the Red Sox's AAA team, was about to be traded to the Baltimore Orioles. Trade rumors are always swirling around professional baseball clubhouses, but this one was true. Anderson was one of the brightest Red Sox outfield stars in the minor leagues, but the Sox wanted Mike Boddicker, the Orioles' star pitcher, to help them win the American League pennant. The Orioles were already out of contention in July, and they were ready to get rid of some of their stars for younger players.

The rumor was that the Orioles wanted not just Brady Anderson, but also a young pitcher from the Red Sox farm system. Schilling wondered to his teammates who that other player might be. Little did he know that he was that player. He looked up at the clubhouse TV in New Britain, Connecticut, as he was preparing to pitch in the second game of a doubleheader there. He saw his name on the TV. He had been traded. "I couldn't believe it," Schilling later told reporters. He went to his friend Todd Pratt, who was on deck and about to hit. "Dude, I just got traded," Schilling said. Pratt replied, "Hang on, I'll go hit a home run for you." When he got to the plate, Pratt hit one of the longest home runs of his life. With that, as of July 29, 1988, Curt Schilling was a Baltimore Oriole.

MAKING IT TO THE BIGS

The Orioles wasted no time in getting Schilling some serious coaching. They sent him to their AA team in Charlotte, North Carolina, for work in the month of August. Unlike the Red Sox, the Orioles had full-time coaches who devoted themselves to teaching pitching prospects, and Schilling responded by winning five of the seven games he pitched.

The minor-league season ended in early September, and Schilling got his second shock in a month. He was called on the phone and told to report to the Orioles. His father's words from eight months earlier were ringing in his ears. He was going to pitch in the major leagues.

The Orioles' manager was Frank Robinson. He had been a legendary player for the Cincinnati Reds and the Orioles, the only player to win the Most Valuable Player award in both the American and National Leagues. He was also the first black manager in baseball history. He was a strong, no-nonsense leader, but he could also be quiet and unassuming. Much later, as manager of the Washington Nationals in 2005, he was asked by one of his players if he had ever played in the major leagues. He assured the player that he had.

When Robinson first met Schilling, two more opposite personalities could not have been found. The reserved Robinson saw in front of him a young, brash pitcher who had an earring and streaks of red and blue in his hair. Schilling also had a big tattoo of a rottweiler on his arm. He had arrived in a new Corvette. Robinson skipped any formal introduction and simply told the new arrival that he would be the starting pitcher on September 7, against the Red Sox. Schilling was thrilled.

Schilling left Robinson's office. He took one of the free tickets given to every player and left it at the ticket office, reserved with his father's name on it. From then on, he would leave a ticket for his father in every single game he ever pitched. Just knowing that there always is an empty seat in the park reserved for the man who had instilled confidence in him makes Schilling feel that his father is with him in some way. He will often look for the seat and imagine his father watching. He had found a way to honor the man who had given him so much.

THE FIRST GAME

On September 7, more than 35,000 fans packed Baltimore's Memorial Stadium for the game against the Red Sox. The Sox were in first place in the American League, and every game was important to them. They drew good crowds wherever they played. Schilling warmed up in the Oriole bullpen, listening to the many fans of both teams and knowing that he would remember this game for the rest of his life. He knew that he had support in the field, led by shortstop Cal Ripken, Jr., who was in the prime of his long career.

When he finally got to the mound, he looked to his catcher, Mickey Tettleton. When he was later asked who the most important person was to a pitcher—the pitching coach, the manager, or the catcher—Schilling would reply, "The catcher." Tettleton was some six years older than Schilling and so may have been a steadying influence. (Tettleton was known for his love of the cereal Froot Loops—he would have that as his nickname for much of his career.) The next person he saw from the mound was Wade Boggs, the leadoff hitter for the Red Sox. Boggs, who would later be elected to the Hall of Fame, was one of the most feared hitters in baseball.

The first player that Curt Schilling faced in his major-league debut in 1988 was Wade Boggs (*above*) of the Boston Red Sox. Boggs was on his way that season to winning his fourth straight American League batting title. In that first showdown, Boggs grounded out to second base.

He had won the American League batting title three years in a row—and would win the 1988 batting title as well. Boggs drew the word "Chai" in the batter's box (a Hebrew word meaning "life") for good luck—he was among the most superstitious players, always drawing the word before he batted, always eating chicken before a game, and always taking exactly 150 ground balls for practice. He looked out at Schilling and scowled.

Schilling took a deep breath and fired his first major-league pitch. Boggs took the pitch for a strike. He swung at the next pitch, bouncing it to second base, and Schilling had his first major-league out. The next batter, Marty Barrett, hit a single, but Schilling got both Dwight Evans and Mike Greenwell out, and left the mound for the Orioles dugout. His first inning was a success.

Schilling pitched well, but he got himself into trouble after hitting a batter in the fifth inning. That led to two Red Sox runs after a big hit by Dwight Evans, and eventually Robinson pulled Schilling from the game after seven innings. The Orioles were losing 3-1, but they later rallied to win the game. Even though Schilling did not get the win, several Red Sox players commented to reporters that the new pitcher was pretty good, with a fastball that moved a little at the end and a decent curveball. Schilling was delighted that his team had beaten the team that had traded him.

IN AND OUT OF THE MONEY

Schilling soon received his first major-league payday—a check for just over $5,000 for two weeks of work. In the minors, he had made less than $5,000 for a year of work, so he felt rich beyond his dreams. His family had not been well-to-do, and this was a welcome change. He cashed the check at a bank and asked the teller to give him all the money in $20 bills. He then took a cab back to his Baltimore hotel room, dumped the money on his bed, and rolled in it. He later said, "I remember thinking, 'This is more money than I'll spend in my entire life. I've made it. Nothing can stop me now.'"

Schilling was 21 and on his own with what he thought was wealth beyond reason. Like many young athletes, he did not know what to do at first except party when he was not pitching. He could now drink in bars. Strangers wanted to be instant friends. He was nowhere near his roots, had lost much of his family, and had no anchor in his life. But he did have free time and lots of money. It was not a healthy combination. Schilling looks back on this time of his life and realizes how immature he was. "I was such a screw-up when I got to the big leagues. I was a total idiot. I ran the nightlife, I drank, I just acted crazy. I did all the stupid things you'd expect from a 21-year-old with money. I can't believe what a dope I was."

Schilling did not pitch well enough to stay in the majors— he was unable or unwilling to make the sacrifices needed to be a great pitcher. He spent most of the next season, 1989, pitching for the Orioles' Class AAA team in Rochester, New York. When he returned to the majors in September, he did not do very well. *Sporting News* reporter Ken Rosenthal wrote about Schilling during this time:

> [The reporter was] watching Curt Schilling in action at the opening of the Hard Rock Café in Washington D.C . . . frantically trying to meet Miss Washington D.C.
>
> "I hear you're a knucklehead," one woman told him. Schilling considered the thought for as long as his attention span would allow (approximately 1.6 seconds in those days), then responded with a goofy grin, "You're right. I am."

Midway through the 1990 season, the Orioles called him up again, and again he found himself in Robinson's office. This time, Schilling had a mohawk haircut to go with his earring and red and blue hair. Robinson lashed into Schilling for his attitude, for not taking pitching seriously enough. "First of all,

Curt Schilling played part of the 1990 season with the Orioles' Class AAA team in Rochester, New York. When Schilling was called back up to the big leagues, manager Frank Robinson chastised him for not taking pitching seriously enough. Robinson told him, too, to get rid of his earring and cut his hair.

you don't throw an inning for me until that earring is gone. Second, I expect you to look and act professional." Robinson later said, "He wasn't a bad kid. He just wanted to be noticed." Schilling did as he was told—he cut his hair and took out the earring. People usually did what Robinson told them to do. Schilling did not change his attitude, though. When he showed up late for a game in September 1990 and then gave up a game-winning home run to the Toronto Blue Jays' Kelly Gruber because he had no idea how to pitch to Gruber, he was yelled at by teammate Joe Price, who called him "clueless." It was a low point in Schilling's career.

TRUE LOVE

Baltimore had a popular cable television channel called Home Team Sports. A beautiful young woman named Shonda Brewer worked there as an associate producer. One day she met Schilling when he invited the Home Team Sports crew to a bar—he was paying the tab, as usual. Friends warned her that Schilling was a partier and had never had a girlfriend for very long. He was trouble, and she should stay away from him. She did, at first. Then they met by chance at a mall and began to talk again. He asked her to dinner, and she agreed. Without his earring and blue hair, he found it easier to get dates with successful and professional women like Shonda. He found her fascinating. She had grown up in Baltimore and was an incredible high school athlete, competing in field hockey, basketball, and fast-pitch softball. She did not grow up wealthy or privileged, and she seemed to devote herself to others more than most people do. Schilling was drawn to her for many reasons besides her obvious beauty.

Over the next few months, and beyond the end of the 1990 season, they began to see more and more of each other. They had similar interests, they both worked in sports, and they both worked in Baltimore. As often happens with young men, the right young woman made a big change in his life. He would later say that many of the steps forward he took in his life after 1990 were in some way related to being involved with Shonda.

Another big change was waiting for Schilling. Even though manager Frank Robinson was against it—he famously said at the end of the 1990 season when asked who the Orioles could trade, "Anybody but Schilling"—Schilling was traded to the Houston Astros in January 1991. The Orioles needed more hitting, and they wanted slugging first baseman Glenn Davis from the Astros. To get him, they had to give up three players, and Schilling was one of them.

Schilling was not happy about being traded. He had only known Shonda for four months, but he was in love and so was she. He was afraid he might lose her if he moved to Houston without her, so he asked her to move with him. She agreed, even though she would be leaving a growing career and she was risking everything on someone she could not have known well. They would be married within 15 months. Schilling had found a new center in his life, and so had Shonda.

GETTING HIT BY A ROCKET

Schilling was now going to his third major-league organization in three years. He had not lived up to his potential and was considered talented but not consistent and prepared. When he opened the 1991 season as a relief pitcher for the Astros, he was awful. Schilling was unable to throw strikes consistently, and relief pitchers who are wild are like football quarterbacks who throw too many interceptions—they usually lose games. He was Wild Thing, the Charlie Sheen character in the movie *Major League*. So, in June 1991, Schilling was sent to the Astros' AAA team in Tucson, Arizona. Pitching coach Bob Cluck told him that he was not getting the right results, even though he had a great fastball. With a great talent comes a great responsibility. Schilling needed to learn that lesson.

In 1991, Curt Schilling was playing for his third major-league organization—the Houston Astros. Again, he did not live up to his potential and was sent to the minor leagues. In the off-season, a meeting with pitching ace Roger Clemens, who chewed out Schilling for wasting his talent, helped to bring about a change in Schilling's attitude.

Curt and Shonda moved near the Houston Astrodome, and after the '91 season, he started to work out in the Astro weight room. Players were supposed to use the exercise equipment and weights during the off-season to stay in shape. Schilling spent most of his time talking to other players. One day in January 1992, Roger Clemens walked into the exercise room. Even though he was a member of the Red Sox, Clemens was welcome there—teams usually open their facilities to other professional athletes as a courtesy. Clemens lived near Houston, and working out in the Astro facility during the winter made sense for him.

Clemens remembered Schilling from the time they had been together with the Red Sox and from the first game Schilling had pitched as an Oriole. He knew how talented Schilling was. When he was Schilling's age, however, Clemens had already won the Cy Young Award (for best pitcher in a league), set a major-league record for striking out 20 batters in a single game, and had won 20 or more games in two seasons. By contrast, Schilling had won four games and lost eleven in the major leagues, and his ERA was over 4.00. One pitcher's major-league results were superb; the other's were below average.

Clemens was called "The Rocket" because he, too, had a devastating fastball. He owed his success to legendary workouts that were sheer torture for someone like Schilling. Clemens had seen Schilling work out. He knew that Schilling did not take it seriously, and such an attitude made him angry. He knew that Schilling was faking his way through a workout. He asked to talk to Schilling. Schilling assumed Clemens wanted to say hello and talk about a new grip for a fastball. Clemens wanted to tell him how he was wasting his talent and showing disrespect for the game. Schilling later told reporters:

> I can't repeat a lot of what he said. . . . He just railed at me.
> He said I was wasting my career and I was cheating the game.

. . . It was one of the three or four most pivotal moments of my career. . . . It was one of those conversations your father has with you when you're going down the wrong path and it saves your life.

Clemens had intervened in Schilling's life. He had hit him with the painful truth, at a time and in a way that changed him instantly. Schilling realized that he had never really prepared for pitching the way a professional prepares for hard work. He had never put all of himself into his job. So, he started his new life that moment—he worked out for the next two hours as if his life depended on it. In many ways, his life did depend on it. Between Shonda giving him a reason to live more responsibly and Clemens acting as the older brother he never had, Schilling regained a "family" just when he needed it.

Unfortunately for the Astros, they did not realize that they had a changed man on their hands, not a confused boy. They traded Schilling to the Philadelphia Phillies on April 2, 1992, for another underachiever, Jason Grimsley. Schilling was never given a chance to show the Astros that he was now ready to take his life seriously. The Phillies would get the new Schilling, and it would land them in a World Series.

Starring in Philly

Philadelphia has always been known as "The City of Brotherly Love," but only a few of its professional athletes see that loving side. The fans and the media are demanding, and Schilling knew what he was walking into. The fans had famously booed a Santa Claus at a Philadelphia Eagles game. They were tough. The Phillies assumed that they knew Schilling—talented, immature, wild in many ways, and a project. When Phillies pitching coach Johnny Podres got to know Schilling, though, he was surprised.

After his meeting with Roger Clemens and after he and Shonda married in 1992, Schilling really had changed. He now worked out, and for real. He did not just do a few sit-ups and call it a day. He now challenged his body to respond. He pestered Podres for tips on pitching and new ways to grip his fastball, slider, curveball, and changeup. He worked on his pitching full time for the first time in his life. His worked on his best pitch, the four-seam fastball. A four-seamer is called that because the pitcher grips the ball with his index and middle fingers touching the seams in four places. It is a power pitch, and Schilling has one of the best four-seamers in baseball history. He and Podres also worked on his location—putting the pitch exactly where the pitcher wants to, usually as far away from the batter as possible without being called a ball. They worked on moving the ball around the strike zone so that a batter did not see the same pitch twice in a row. Keeping a batter off-balance was the key to success.

They also worked on his windup. Schilling had been both a relief pitcher and a starter, and he had changed his windup several times. Relief pitchers often do not use a full windup so they can help keep base runners closer to the bags and less able to steal. Having a consistent windup is a key to pitching well. Schilling was learning and relearning everything about pitching a baseball.

Finally, Schilling started a practice that he continues to this day. He began to take notes on batters and on what pitches he should use against them. He later said to reporters:

> I have notes on hitters, notes on umpires; everything I need to be ready to pitch on the day I pitch. . . . There's no reason why I shouldn't be able to go out and win if I throw strikes. . . . I believe I'm better prepared than any hitter I face. I try to prepare so thoroughly that there's never a situation that arises in a game that surprises me. . . . Surprise is not a good thing.

This was the new Curt Schilling. He was better both physically and mentally. He was ready to begin the best years of his professional life.

THE 1992 SEASON: A TURNING POINT

When the Phillies started the 1992 season, they had high hopes. Soon, however, many of the starting pitchers were injured or had sore arms. By the middle of May, the Phillies were desperate enough to give this new pitcher named Schilling a chance to start regularly. Until then, Schilling had been appearing as a relief pitcher. On May 19, manager Jim Fregosi and pitching coach Podres put Schilling into the lineup as the starting pitcher against the Astros. Just as the Orioles had thrown him against his old team, the Red Sox, so the Phillies thought he would have a grudge against the team that had just traded him.

Schilling warmed up in the bullpen, working on smoothing out his windup and going through all the pitches he wanted to throw. He would release the ball at exactly the same point in his motion. He would always throw at "¾," meaning his arm would be halfway between sidearm and straight over the top when he threw. He had a plan on how to approach each hitter. He was prepared. Finally, he walked out to the mound, looked around at his infield teammates, and faced the lead-off batter—Craig Biggio. Biggio was one of the scrappiest hitters in baseball, but on this day against this new Schilling, he did not stand a chance. The first pitch was on the outside part of home plate, a called strike. The second pitch was on the inside part of the plate, for strike two. Schilling put extra on the third pitch, and it was past Biggio before he could get his bat around. Strike three. Veterans Stadium erupted with delight. Who *was* this pitcher?

Schilling overpowered and confused most of the batters he faced that day. He moved the fastball in and out, mixing it with sliders (a fast curveball). After six innings, his team was ahead 4-0, and Fregosi thought it was time to bring in a relief pitcher, since Schilling had not pitched this many innings in a game in a long time. The Phillies won the game, 4-3, and Schilling was the winning pitcher.

Curt Schilling throws at "¾"—halfway between sidearm and straight over the top—as seen here in a game with the Philadelphia Phillies on May 24, 1992. Five days earlier, the Phillies began to use Schilling as a starting pitcher after he spent the first weeks of the season as a reliever.

Instead of heading for the nearest bar after the game, Schilling began to think about his next game. He pitched well again. The 1992 season continued with Schilling pitching better than he ever had, and he ended the year with an ERA of 2.35, fourth-best in the National League. Schilling won 14 games and lost 11 for a team that only won 70 games. He was finally a major-league starting pitcher. It felt wonderful.

1993: THE LEAGUE CHAMPIONS

Many National League batters felt that Schilling would not surprise them in 1993. They thought that he would return to his old, inconsistent ways. The team had finished in last place, and Schilling had had a fluke year. This year, batters would catch up to him.

The National League was wrong. Schilling pitched even better in 1993, winning 16 games and losing 7. Many Phillies who were injured the previous year were now healthy, and soon Tommy Greene and Terry Mulholland were pitching well. John Kruk hit well as the first baseman, and outfielder Lenny Dykstra provided a spark that ignited each and every player. The Phillies took over first place in the National League East early in the year and never gave it up.

They made it to the National League Championship Series against the Atlanta Braves. Most people picked the Braves to go to the World Series, and Atlanta had both good pitching and good hitting. Fregosi chose Schilling to start the first game of the championship series. For most of the country, that decision was a surprise—few people outside Philadelphia knew who this young pitcher was. On that day, Schilling became well known. As Schilling would later say, before the 1993 National League Championship Series, he was "a loud nobody. Then I became a loud somebody." Buying a red Lamborghini from José Canseco also drew attention to him.

The opposing pitcher was Steve Avery, a first-round draft choice who had been a major-league hero at 21. He was supposed to be the better pitcher. Veterans Stadium was rocking when Schilling took the mound. By the time he finished the first inning, striking out Otis Nixon, Jeff Blauser, and Ron Gant, some thought that the stadium was in danger of collapsing from the foot-stomping. When Schilling struck out the fourth and fifth batters as well in the second inning, fans outside the park might have thought an earthquake had struck Philadelphia. He had just set a championship-series record for consecutive strikeouts.

Avery gave up a double and a single to the first batters who faced him and was down 1-0 before he knew what hit him. Schilling threw 148 pitches that day in eight innings, striking out 10 and leading the team to a 4-3 victory. He had given up only two hits in 13 at-bats to the heart of the Braves lineup—Ron Gant, David Justice, and Fred McGriff. McGriff would later give Schilling a high compliment—he said Schilling was "inside, outside, up, down. It's really tough to zone in."

Schilling met reporters after the game:

> I can't remember ever pitching better than that. I give a lot of credit to catcher Darren Daulton. We were pretty much in sync all night, and especially after the five strikeouts. I've been in situations before where I've had good adrenaline early only to see it go away. You have to protect yourself from a letdown.

The only batter to hit Schilling hard had been Avery, the pitcher. Schilling later said that his father would have been on him about that. As usual, Schilling had left a ticket for his father, and after this sweet victory he must have thought a good deal about what his father might have said to him.

The Phillies got a big boost from their opening-game victory and went on to defeat the Braves in six games. Schilling pitched well again in Game 5 and was named the Most

Valuable Player of the championship series. The country now knew who he was.

THE 1993 WORLD SERIES

The Toronto Blue Jays were ready for Schilling in the 1993 World Series, and they beat him in the first game, 8-5. It was the biggest loss of his young career, and many waited to see if and how he would bounce back. In Game 4, the day before Schilling pitched again, the Phillies lost, 15-14. The game lasted more than four hours, and the Phillies used most of their relief pitchers. Catcher Darren Daulton joked that for the fifth game Schilling should try to keep the Blue Jays under 14 runs. If the Blue Jays won Game 5, they would win the World Series.

Schilling started Game 5 strong, pitching in the mid-90–mile-per-hour range. His fastball was moving, and the Blue Jays were in trouble. By the eighth inning, though, Schilling's fastball had slowed down to 86 miles per hour (138 kilometers per hour), and he was running out of energy. There were no relief pitchers to come in and save the game—they had all been used up in Game 4. It was up to Schilling. He used his head. He changed speeds. He changed locations. And, he needed some luck. When Rickey Henderson hit a vicious line drive in the eighth inning with a runner at third base and the Phillies leading, 2-0, the ball could easily have gone through for a hit and a run. Instead, it hit Schilling on the leg, and he picked it up and threw it home to get the runner in a rundown. Schilling stayed in the game and kept throwing strikes. The Phillies went on to win the game and stay alive. Schilling had been brilliant—and tough.

Toronto outfielder Joe Carter ended the 1993 World Series with a walk-off three-run home run in the ninth inning of the sixth game. The Phillies had lost, but they had come further than anyone thought possible, and they now had a star pitcher—Curt Schilling.

Curt Schilling greeted teammate Jim Eisenreich after Eisenreich's three-run home run in Game 2 of the 1993 World Series. In Game 5, the congratulations would all be turned Schilling's way. With the Phillies bullpen depleted, Schilling pitched a gutsy complete game against the Toronto Blue Jays to keep his team alive in the Series.

1994: DISASTER IN PHILLY AND IN BASEBALL

Many major-league players are superstitious, and some believe in curses. The year 1994 was, by all accounts, a cursed year for Schilling and for Major League Baseball. Instead of starting out strong and taking over where they left off, the Phillies flopped. Schilling's arm hurt, and then he injured his knee and needed surgery. Many other Phillies also went out with injuries.

On August 12, 1994, professional baseball players went on strike. The strike lasted 232 days and led to the cancellation of 920 games, including the 1994 World Series. Baseball became the first sport in history to lose its postseason. Some estimate that $1 billion was lost by the players and the team owners, the two sides in the battle. It was the longest and costliest work stoppage in the history of sports. When it ended, neither side had given in. The only change was that hundreds of thousands of fans had lost interest in the game. Two world wars, the Great Depression, and earthquakes had never stopped the World Series. Greed and selfishness did.

Finally, when some owners said they would use replacement players for the 1995 season, a federal judge ruled that the owners had violated U.S. labor laws. Soon both sides agreed to reinstate the contract conditions that existed before the strike. The long and costly strike was a huge waste of time and stands as a model of what not to do during labor negotiations.

1995–2000: SERVICE TO OTHERS

Schilling now entered a period in his life when what he did off the field mattered as much as what he did on the field. His arm and shoulder were hurting, and he was kept out of many games in 1995 and 1996. He had always wanted to finish every game he started, and the innings had taken their toll. He re-signed in 1996 with the Phillies, but for much less money than rival star pitchers like Roger Clemens of the Red Sox, Greg Maddux of the Braves, and Randy Johnson of the

Mariners. He felt loyal to the team, and the Phillies had stuck with him when he was hurt.

The Schillings began to raise money to combat Lou Gehrig's disease (formally known as amyotrophic lateral sclerosis, or ALS), a deadly illness that affects the body's nervous system and is named after the Yankee great who died from the disease. The Phillies had been instrumental in helping the Greater Philadelphia Chapter of the ALS Association, and Curt and Shonda Schilling threw themselves into the organization. Earlier in his Phillies career, Schilling had formed "Curt's Pitch for ALS," in which he agreed to donate $100 per strikeout and $1,000 per win to the organization. Fans, too, could make contributions. By 2000, the Schillings had raised $1.7 million this way.

At the end of the 1995 season, Schilling was awarded the prestigious Lou Gehrig Memorial Award, given to the major-league player who does the most to support worthy causes off the field. Schilling joined such winners as Hank Aaron (1970), Cal Ripken, Jr. (1992), and Don Mattingly (1993). The Schillings felt so strongly about helping support the fight against ALS that they named their first child Gehrig (born on May 27, 1995). Schilling was now a father, and his maturity showed even more.

When a doctor found a lesion in his mouth during a routine exam in March 1998, Schilling was told that he must stop using smokeless tobacco or risk having mouth cancer. He began to speak out against young people using smokeless tobacco, something he knew more about now. He had used "chew" since high school, as had many baseball players. He wanted to get the word out about its risks. He had "dipped" without thinking every day for many years. That would come to an end now.

Soon the Schillings found one more cause to support. Shonda was diagnosed with a deadly kind of skin cancer, melanoma, in early 2001. She had to undergo several surgeries, and

(continues on page 55)

☆ ☆ ☆ ☆ ☆

LOU GEHRIG

When Ludwig Heinrich Gehrig was born in the Yorkville section of New York City on June 3, 1903, his German immigrant
parents were struggling. His mother cleaned houses and took
in laundry to support the family when his father lost jobs as an
ironworker and janitor because of epilepsy. The couple, though,
had high hopes for their son, later called "Louis Henry" and
then just "Lou"—hopes that Lou would go to a good college and
become an architectural engineer.

Lou grew rapidly into a tall, strong, and handsome teenager,
excelling at football and baseball. When his high school team
traveled to Chicago to play that city's best team, he hit a home
run out of Cubs Park (now Wrigley Field) that went farther than
those hit by most major leaguers. Yet his football talent was
what attracted the most notice when he was a teenager—he was
an almost unstoppable force as a fullback. So, he won a football
scholarship to Columbia University in New York.

His parents' plans for him changed on April 18, 1923 (the
day Yankee Stadium opened), when a scout for the New York
Yankees saw Gehrig strike out 17 batters from Williams College
during a game at Columbia. It wasn't Gehrig's pitching that
impressed the scout. It was his hitting. Within days, Gehrig
signed a Yankee contract. The rest is baseball history: He
played in 2,130 consecutive games (a record only broken
by Cal Ripken, Jr. in 1995), despite having multiple broken
bones over that period—X-rays late in his career show he had
17 "healed" fractures in his hands. He had a lifetime batting
average of .340, and averaged 147 RBIs per season (a record).
He is in baseball's truly elite group of all-time all-stars,

considered to be the best first baseman ever to play professional baseball.

When his enormous skills declined suddenly in 1939, he underwent six days of tests at the Mayo Clinic in Minnesota. On June 19, 1939, on his thirty-sixth birthday, he was diagnosed as having a rare and incurable disease that destroys the nervous system but leaves the mind intact. Muscles weaken when nerve cells in the brain cannot activate muscle movement, and paralysis eventually sets in. The disease is amyotrophic lateral sclerosis (ALS). It was soon to be known as "Lou Gehrig's disease."

On July 4, 1939, 62,000 fans at Yankee Stadium stood and cheered and wept during a farewell speech Gehrig gave. He called himself "the luckiest man on the face of the earth" because of the love and support he had been given by his family, teammates, and fans. Many have called it one of the shining moments in American sports history. On June 2, 1941, Gehrig died. Flags flew at half-staff in several parts of the country. He was America's image of itself—strong, humble, honest, and hard-working. He was mourned by millions, including President Franklin Roosevelt.

To this day, there is no known cause of ALS, and therefore no cure. Recently, a drug named Rilutek has been developed that seems to slow the progress of the disease. With revolutionary advances in linking specific genes and proteins with specific diseases, and with help from foundations like those funded by the Schillings, the 30,000 Americans suffering from ALS have more hope now than they did even a few years ago.

During Curt's time with the Philadelphia Phillies, Curt and Shonda Schilling became active in the fight against amyotrophic lateral sclerosis (ALS), also known as Lou Gehrig's disease. Here, they were the hosts of a fund-raiser in Philadelphia in November 2001 with their children *(from left)* Gabriella, Gehrig, and Grant.

(continued from page 51)
Schilling said later, "It made me stronger, a better husband and a better father." Together, they started the Curt and Shonda Schilling Melanoma Foundation to raise money to treat and raise awareness about the disease. The foundation has been very successful and has helped save many lives.

HEADING FOR A NEW TEAM

When he was healthy, Schilling continued to do well. He had had successful shoulder surgery in late 1995, performed by Dr. Craig Morgan. After recovering, he could actually throw harder than he did before the surgery. Schilling's record was 17–11 in 1997, and 15–14 in 1998. (In both years, the Phillies had losing records.) He had 319 strikeouts in 1997 and 300 in 1998. He had worked $268^2/3$ innings in 1998 and thrown 4,213 pitches. He led the major leagues in complete games (15), the most since Roger Clemens completed 18 games in 1987. Schilling was rightfully proud of his work ethic, of completing games:

> I approach the game as mine. With pitch counts and all the junk that comes with being a young pitcher in the '90s, it's [complete games] not something a lot of teams are interested in pushing their kids to do. They don't care to have them learn what it's like to get a guy out for a fourth time without your good stuff.

All the pitching, though, took its toll. In 1999, he went 15–6 but missed most of the last two months of the season because of shoulder trouble. Finally, in December, tests showed that his throwing shoulder was partly torn—or at least the muscles were stretched out of shape. He would need surgery again.

By 2000, Schilling had recovered from his surgery and was doing better. The Phillies, though, did not have the ability to put together a championship team, and Schilling was getting restless. He had come close to winning a World Series in 1993 but had not been close to getting back to one. It is a player's ultimate dream, and one Schilling could not give up. He even had some famous confrontations with the owners of the Phillies, publicly questioning whether the team was trying hard enough to attract the best players and pitchers. In mid-2000, he told the Phillies that he would be willing to be traded to the Arizona Diamondbacks. All of baseball knew that the Diamondbacks were on the verge of being great, especially after they signed Randy Johnson, a 6-foot-10 (208-centimeter) giant who scared many a professional hitter. Schilling reasoned that, if he could go to a team with another star pitcher, his chances of winning a World Series ring would greatly increase. He was right. On July 26, 2000, Schilling became a Diamondback, and he moved back to the state he loved—Arizona.

The Schillings had been lucky enough to have two more children during this time, Gabriella in 1997 and Grant in 1999. Garrison, their fourth child, would be born soon, in 2002. His growing family meant the world to Schilling. He was now a completely changed man, and he only needed to be physically healthy to achieve his lifelong goal of winning a world championship. He also needed one other thing—a teammate who was a pitcher of equal skill and tenacity.

A Diamondback Dynamic Duo

When both Randy Johnson and Curt Schilling started the season for the 2001 Arizona Diamondbacks, baseball insiders knew that something special would happen. Johnson was the most feared pitcher in baseball. When he glared at a batter and then seemed to release the ball only a few feet from home plate from his long left arm, no batter could plant himself firmly. He made batters nervous. Schilling was now healthy, and Johnson was in peak form. They became one of the most dynamic pitching duos in baseball history. Schilling and Johnson inspired each other during the season. Schilling's record was a remarkable 22–6, Johnson's was 21–6, and they both had plenty of strikeouts—Johnson had 372, and Schilling had 293. The team won the National League West and was going to the postseason.

TRAGEDY STRIKES

On Tuesday, September 11, 2001, four commercial airliners were hijacked, and two were flown into the World Trade Center in New York City. One was flown into the Pentagon in Arlington County, Virginia, and the fourth plane crashed into a field in Somerset County, Pennsylvania. More than 3,000 people were killed. The Diamondbacks heard the news as America did, slowly and painfully. Suddenly, their season seemed both less and more important.

The attacks affected everyone. Many, including Schilling, were deeply moved by the heroism of the rescue workers at the World Trade Center. Schilling wrote an open letter to the families of the workers, letting them know that professional athletes were humbled by the sacrifices of their husbands and wives, who were true heroes.

Later, when the Diamondbacks traveled to New York City to be in the World Series, their first stop was at Ground Zero. New York City officials asked that a member of the Diamondbacks speak to 100 workers at a police command center, and Schilling stepped forward. He was the team's emotional leader. Sergeant Lisa Gong of the New York Police Department described to reporters the effect of Schilling's impromptu speech:

> I have not heard a more eloquent speaker. Everyone was moved, not only by his words but the way he delivered them. What he had to say was pertinent, well-intentioned, and well-received. He offered his sympathy and compassion and empathy, all in one paragraph. It couldn't have been more than two minutes in length.

Workers later came out of the pile of rubble at Ground Zero to introduce themselves to Schilling and his teammates. Men passed Schilling their cellphones so he could talk to their families. It is difficult to make a New York City police officer or construction worker cry. That day at the command post and at Ground Zero, there were many faces streaked with tears.

After 9/11, the Diamondbacks and baseball officials knew that the season must go on. The Diamondbacks had to play the St. Louis Cardinals in the National League Division Series. Schilling was given the start in Game 1 by manager Bob Brenly, and he made his manager look like a genius. He gave up only three hits, and the D-Backs won 1-0. Schilling and Johnson led Arizona to victory against the Cards and then defeated the Atlanta Braves, four games to one, to win the National League Championship Series. Atlanta manager Bobby Cox said of Schilling, "He's so much better than he was with the Phillies. He can spot all his pitches now." Schilling's control had never been better. He and his team were going to the 2001 World Series.

THE 2001 WORLD SERIES—BEST EVER?

The New York Yankees had won three straight world championships and were good enough to win the American League pennant again. With the tragedy of 9/11, a city in shock turned to its beloved team for some distraction and relief. The Yankees had great pitching, led by Roger Clemens, Andy Pettitte, and Mike Mussina, and great hitting and leadership, spearheaded by the incomparable Derek Jeter. Just two weeks before the 2001 World Series began, in the American League Division Series, Jeter turned in one of the most spectacular plays in postseason history. He had, out of nowhere, run at full speed across the pitcher's mound, leaped into the air, caught an off-target throw from the outfield, and in one motion flipped the ball toward home plate to the Yankee catcher (the veteran Jorge Posada). Posada tagged out Jason Giambi of the Oakland A's as he was trying to score, and one of the most famous plays in postseason history became an instant legend. Teams simply do not practice having a third cut-off man make a play. Players had never seen a play like that—ESPN listed

In Game 1 of the 2001 World Series, Curt Schilling's fastball was clocked at 97 miles per hour. The Arizona Diamondbacks won that game against the Yankees 9-1. The World Series, though, would be a close contest, its outcome decided in the ninth inning of the final game.

"The Flip" as one the most memorable sports moments of the past 25 years.

The Yankees had won 26 world championships. The Diamondbacks had won none. When a reporter asked Schilling if he was worried about the Yankees' mystique and aura, he replied, "When you use words like 'mystique' and 'aura,' those are dancers in a nightclub. These are not things we concern ourselves with on the ball field." The reporters had to laugh, and the team seemed looser because of Schilling's attitude.

The 2001 World Series opened in Arizona, with a temperature of 94 degrees at game time. Schilling started Game 1, and his fastball was blazing, clocked at 97 miles per hour (156 kilometers per hour). He was almost unhittable. The Diamondbacks rolled over the Yankees, 9-1. Johnson started Game 2 and shut the Yankees out. Yankee fans talked about the two-headed monster that was the D-back pitching staff.

The Yankees, though, won Games 3, 4, and 5 in Yankee Stadium. Game 3 was won by Roger Clemens, the same man who had helped turn Schilling's career around. Game 4 was played under a full moon on Halloween, highlighted by a Jeter walk-off home run in the tenth inning—the first walk-off home run of his life, and it happened just after midnight on November 1, a Halloween present to all Yankee fans. Jeter was instantly nicknamed "Mr. November." When Scott Brosius hit a two-out, two-run homer in the ninth inning to tie Game 5, which the Yankees won in the twelfth inning, baseball historians began to call the 2001 World Series one of the best ever. Just when the country had needed a distraction from its fears and worries, two baseball teams were providing it. The Yankees now led three games to two. The Series returned to Arizona. Many thought it was already over.

Johnson pitched a great game in Game 6, as Arizona pummeled New York, 15-2. Game 7 featured a classic pitching matchup, Schilling against Clemens. Before the Series even started, Schilling had said, "If I get the ball in the seventh game, we win." Some likened it to quarterback Joe Namath's brash prediction that his Jets would win Super Bowl III. Schilling and Clemens pitched brilliantly, and the Diamondbacks led 1-0 after six innings. The Yankees scored a run in the seventh inning, and in the eighth inning, Yankee second baseman Alfonso Soriano hit a home run on a pitch that was so low some still insist it hit the dirt first. Schilling later said that only burying the pitch would have made it lower. The Yankees took the lead, 2-1, and Schilling was removed for a relief pitcher. That reliever, Miguel Batista, was replaced one out later by none other than Randy Johnson. The Yankees did not score again.

The Yankees gave the ball to Mariano Rivera, their legendary relief pitcher, for the ninth inning. Their twenty-seventh championship was three outs away. Schilling watched intently from the dugout. He did not want to miss a minute. The Diamondbacks rallied. When Luis Gonzalez's broken-bat single flared into center field for a hit, scoring Jay Bell with the winning run, the Yankees were stunned, and the D-backs flowed onto the field. "Celebration" rocked through the domed stadium. Arizona became the first team ever to rally from a ninth-inning deficit in Game 7 of a World Series. The home team had won every game, and the country had been treated to a brief but real break from tragic world events.

REAPING THE REWARDS

The dynamic duo of Johnson and Schilling won co-Most Valuable Player awards for the 2001 World Series. It was the first time in baseball history that two pitchers had been honored as co-winners. They deserved it. Schilling had gone 4-0 in six postseason starts, with a minuscule ERA of 1.12. He had completed three of the games, and pitched two with only three days' rest. In $48^{1}/_3$ innings, he had struck out 56 and walked six. It was a performance for the ages.

Major League Baseball gave Schilling the prestigious Roberto Clemente Award, for the player who shows both exceptional involvement in community work and extraordinary contributions to his team. The honor meant more to Schilling than most because his father's favorite player was Clemente, the Pittsburgh Pirates legend. His father had cried when Clemente died in a plane crash, one of the very few times Schilling saw that side of his father. The first major-league game that Schilling ever went to was Clemente's last game.

★ ★ ★ ★ ★ ★
THE ROBERTO CLEMENTE AWARD

One of the most prestigious awards in baseball is the Roberto Clemente Award, originally called the "Commissioner's Award" but renamed for Roberto Clemente after his death in 1972. The annual award honors the major-league player who has done the most for his community and has been a goodwill ambassador for baseball. Many great players have been honored with the award, including Sammy Sosa of the Chicago Cubs in 1998 and Carlos Delgado of the New York Mets in 2006.

Clemente was born in Carolina, Puerto Rico, on August 18, 1934, and played 18 seasons with the Pittsburgh Pirates, from 1955 to 1972. He was an incredible force in baseball—he was a four-time National League batting champion, had a lifetime batting average of .317, and finished his career with exactly 3,000 hits, the eleventh player to reach that many. He won 12 Gold Glove awards (tied with Willie Mays for the most ever by an outfielder). Clemente is one of only four players in major-league history to have more than 10 Gold Glove awards and a lifetime batting average above .300. He was the first Hispanic player voted into the Baseball Hall of Fame—what Jackie Robinson did for African-American players in opening up professional baseball, Clemente did for Latino players.

In late December 1972, Nicaragua was hit by a devastating earthquake. Clemente always spent much of his time during the off-season involved in charity work. On New Year's Eve, he coordinated the loading of a private plane with supplies for the earthquake relief effort. The plane crashed off the coast of Isla Verde, Puerto Rico, and Clemente's body was never recovered. The Clemente Award was named to honor him.

The Arizona Diamondbacks' two pitching aces—Curt Schilling and Randy Johnson—held up the World Series Most Valuable Player trophy after Arizona's victory in Game 7 on November 4, 2001. The two men were named co-recipients of the award—the first time two pitchers had shared the honor.

Sporting News, an important source of news about baseball and other sports, gave Schilling its much-publicized "Sportsman of the Year" award on December 17, 2001. In a moving article about Schilling's life, writer Ken Rosenthal summarized Schilling's impact on the sport and on the country in 2001:

The 2001 postseason was Schilling's masterpiece, a career-defining display of his vast skill, fierce will, and exhaustive preparation. . . . Whether on the mound or at home, in his community or at Ground Zero, he is everything that fans want their superstars to be. A gifted athlete who maximizes his talent. A devoted husband and father in times of crisis. A philanthropist obsessed with finding a cure for a fatal disease. A patriot willing not only to be a spokesman but the conscience of his sport. . . . Funny how some athletes just figure it out. Look at Schilling now, and it's difficult to remember him as an immature goofball. It's easy to say, "There goes the Sportsman of the Year."

Schilling was also the winner of the Hutch Award, named for Fred Hutchinson, a former manager who had died of cancer. The award went to a baseball player who had overcome some adversity in their lives and succeeded. Former winners included Mickey Mantle of the Yankees (1965) and Sandy Koufax of the Dodgers (1966) as well as David Cone (Yankees, 1998) and Craig Biggio (Astros, 2005). All, including Schilling, had overcome serious injuries.

THE SECRETS OF SUCCESS

After the 2001 World Series, the baseball world learned about Schilling's preparation for each game. In 1997, he had begun to send copies of his game videos to a company in Los Angeles, which would edit the tapes and send back a CD-ROM with clips of his pitches, catalogued by hitter. He can view his pitches by type and location and get a "book" on every hitter he faces. He breaks down every game into every at-bat and every pitch. He is a perfectionist.

The baseball world heard the story of how Schilling meets with his catcher and coaches before the game to see how to play each hitter. He might want the infield to shift when he has two strikes on a hitter, or one outfielder to move over when he is planning to throw curveballs to a particular batter. He will sometimes reposition fielders from the mound—leaving nothing to chance. If he throws the pitch where he wants, and the hitter reacts the way he expects, the ball will be going where he thinks it will. The left fielder whose hit won the World Series, Luis Gonzalez, told reporters, "He has a great idea of what he's doing. You listen to him and go with it. If you get burned, he'll come up to you and tell you, 'Don't worry about it. It's my fault for missing a spot.'"

Newspaper articles were written about Schilling's routines. He leaves for the park at the same time each day, dresses at the same time, and stretches at the same time. He lets his children choose his pitching-day wardrobe at the beginning of the year and wears the same outfit each day he pitches. For 2001, it was a pale green shirt, tan slacks, and brown shoes. Gonzalez told Schilling that he was going to burn the outfit at the end of the season, but the season kept going on and on.

Experts now used Schilling as a poster child for proper pitching mechanics. He always had good balance when he was winding up, holding the glove close to his body. He hides the ball well so batters cannot see it. His well-developed quadricep muscles help drive him toward home plate; his stride foot also moves directly toward it. He transfers his weight to his front leg smoothly and is ready to field a ball at the end of his delivery. He does not fall off to the left or right side after delivery. His eyes stay focused on his target. He was picture perfect in his mechanics.

Pitching experts had always studied Schilling's varieties of fastball—the sinker, the cutter that moves away from right-handed batters, and the four-seamer that stays straight but seems to rise. Now they studied his ability to outthink the batter. When a batter thought he had picked up a pattern—say, Schilling tending to pitch a fastball to the outside corner of the plate on the first or second pitch—the batter would "learn" and begin to anticipate the pitch. Somehow, though, Schilling would vary the pattern just as the batter picked it up—giving the advantage back to Schilling. It was a chess game of moves and countermoves. It was a thinking man's game.

All the routines, training, thinking, and preparations had paid off. Schilling, however, had two more secrets to his success. One was that he was a man of enormous emotions. "Before I pitch any game, from spring training to Game 7 of the World Series, I'm scared to death. But that's the drive. That's where I get it. That's the motivation. The feeling after I lose a game, I can't describe how miserable, and the elation I feel after I pitch well is so much less than the bad." The other key to his success was that both Schillings were now people of deep religious faith. They had been "born again," and their lives were filled with a deeper meaning and purpose.

MOVING NORTH

Schilling carried over his superb pitching from 2001 to 2002. His record in 2002 was 23–7, and he struck out more than 300 hitters for the third time in his career. He became one of the very few players in baseball history who had struck out 300 or more batters in a season with two different teams. Nolan Ryan had done it (with the Angels and the Rangers), Randy Johnson had, too (with the Mariners and the Diamondbacks), and Pedro Martínez had as well (with the Expos and the Red Sox). Now, Schilling joined this elite group. These were four of the best pitchers in modern major-league history.

He and Johnson were again arguably the two best pitchers in baseball in 2002, certainly the best two on the same team. But the Diamondbacks had lost some key players after their championship year, as teams often do. They lost to the Cardinals in the first round of the 2002 play-offs, proving once again how temporary world championships are.

Schilling had a nightmare 2003 season. An emergency appendectomy kept him out of the early part of the year, and a broken pitching hand benched him for June and part of July. Trying to adjust and come back from the hand injury, he strained his left knee, the leg he lands on after a pitch. While trying to pitch through that pain, his "perfect" mechanics were

His hand wrapped, Curt Schilling watched from the dugout as Arizona finished its game on May 30, 2003, against the San Diego Padres. He was pulled from the game after his pitching hand was hit twice—once in the first inning and again in the seventh. A few days later, it was discovered that Schilling had suffered a hairline fracture in the hand. During the 2003 season, Schilling was plagued by injuries that affected his mechanics.

thrown off and he strained his hamstring and groin. Nothing went well, and each injury caused another. Baseball historians remembered the famous case of pitcher Dizzy Dean, who fractured his big toe and changed his motion to minimize the pain, only to hurt his arm with the changed motion, cutting short his brilliant career. When told that he had fractured his toe, Dean had famously said that he had not, he had only broken it.

The Diamondbacks missed the play-offs in 2003 and looked for a way to save themselves some money. Schilling was also restless, having accomplished one mission in Arizona and now seeking another. The D-backs agreed to trade Schilling, to get rid of his large salary—some $10 million a year. Schilling stated that he wanted to head back East. Soon, only one team was in the running—the Boston Red Sox, the team that originally drafted him. The circle of baseball life had been completed.

Red Sox general manager Theo Epstein and team president Larry Lucchino spent part of the 2003 Thanksgiving holiday with the Schillings, nailing down the terms of his contract. Lucchino apologized for the Orioles trading him away so many years ago—Lucchino had been CEO of the Orioles at the time. Schilling had become most interested in the Red Sox when he realized just how passionate their fans were. He went to a Red Sox fan Web site message board and stayed until 2:30 A.M. He also knew that the team was hiring Terry Francona, someone Schilling had played for in Philadelphia and respected, as its new manager. On November 30, 2003, Schilling became a member of a team he would help guide to its championship destiny. He said, "I like the thought of playing in the biggest rivalry in sports in front of some incredible fans. The Yankee-Red Sox rivalry transcends sports." He added, "I guess this means I hate the Yankees now."

Making a Promise and Keeping It

Curt Schilling took Boston by storm. Only two months into the 2004 season, he was seen on area television with Shonda and his four children as part of an ad campaign for New England Ford dealers. His face appeared on a Reebok billboard near Boston's Fenway Park and then on more billboards around the city. He could be seen practicing his Boston accent on television for another company and was making regular radio appearances on WROR with morning DJs Loren and Wally. Actor Ben Affleck kidded him at an April luncheon for the Boston Red Sox Foundation, "Curt, I think there are one or two things you're not currently promoting in town. Are there?" He was everywhere.

The fans loved it, because recent Red Sox stars had been much more introverted—Nomar Garciaparra was a very private person, Pedro Martínez was temperamental, and Manny Ramírez refused to talk to the press. Manny was being Manny. Schilling was in chatrooms, on talk shows, and seemed to be enjoying all the attention he was getting. His teammates in Arizona had taken to calling him "Red Light" after the light that comes on when a camera is rolling. Schilling always seemed to love the cameras.

He also knew, though, that being so public was a way to have a more normal life. Schilling had learned that the more people could see and meet him and his family, the more they would give him his privacy when he needed it. "I'm not different from anybody else, except for my ability to throw a baseball and my paycheck," he said. "By letting people see you and your family, they see that, and they become comfortable around you."

2004: THE SEASON AND THE COMEBACK

Schilling was well aware that what happened on the field was really what counted. He promised that he would bring a world championship to the Sox. He knew that being part of a pitching combination was a key to that championship—it had worked in Arizona, and he needed it to work here in Boston. The Red Sox had one of the other supreme pitchers in baseball—Pedro Martínez. Schilling went out of his way to praise him: "Pedro is the ace of the staff. . . . He'll be the ace of the staff three years from now, when we're still together [a prediction that did not turn out to be true—Martínez was traded to the New York Mets in 2005]. . . . The guy is a multiple Cy Young Award winner, the best pitcher in the American League." Schilling knew that superstars could get territorial when another star came into their clubhouse. He would defer to Martínez, outwardly at least. It would take both of them, and many others, to fulfill his championship promise.

Curt Schilling pitches in the first inning of his first game against the New York Yankees as a Red Sox player. Schilling pitched more than six innings in the game on April 17, 2004, and earned the victory.

What neither Schilling nor anyone else knew was that Boston had a third pitcher who would have a career-best postseason, one of the best postseasons in history—Derek Lowe.

Martínez, Lowe, and knuckleballer Tim Wakefield had taken the Red Sox close to the 2003 World Series, but the Yankees, their bitter rivals, had beaten them in the American League Championship Series, a famous series that featured Yankee coach Don Zimmer and Martínez in a brawl. Beating the Yankees was the key to the Red Sox winning their first world championship since 1918, and everyone knew it.

On April 17, 2004, Schilling faced the Yankees for the first time as a Red Sox player. He pitched well—more than six innings—and won the game. It was an important first step. But he lost a crucial game against them in July, and he was now 13–5. When he finished the regular season at 21–6, Red Sox fans knew that he had done well but that his season was just beginning.

The Red Sox finished behind the Yankees in the American League East but won the wild-card race. So, they would play the Anaheim Angels in the American League Division Series. Schilling started the first game, and no one thought much about it when he twisted his ankle coming off the mound to field a ball. He believed that the injury was minor, and so did everyone else. The Red Sox swept the Angels and headed to New York to face the Yankees.

Baseball fans know the story well. Red Sox fans know the story by heart. The big first loss to the Yankees in Game 1 of the American League Championship Series, 10-7, when Schilling pitched poorly and it became clear that the ankle injury was more serious than anyone realized. The losses in Games 2 and 3, the latter a 19-8 embarrassment, that became a low point. No team in history had come back from being down three games to none. Finally, being behind in the ninth inning of Game 4, just about dead. The miracle rally, with Yankee reliever Mariano Rivera sprawling helplessly on the mound as Bill Mueller knocked in Dave Roberts with the tying run. David Ortiz's twelfth-inning home run to win Game 4 for the Sox, and his game-winning bloop single in the fourteenth inning the next night. Ortiz singlehandedly destroying the Yankees in key at-bats. Schilling's Game 6, and the bloody sock. The final victory, 10-3 in Game 7, Johnny Damon's grand slam, sending the Red Sox to the World Series.

THE 2004 WORLD SERIES

Baseball fans tend to concentrate only on the remarkable Red Sox-Yankee championship series when they discuss the 2004 season. But the World Series with the St. Louis Cardinals had its own drama. The Cardinals were a powerful team, one that would win the World Series only two years later.

Game 1 was played at Fenway Park because the American League had won the 2004 All-Star Game, and by rule the winning league's team becomes the World Series home team. It made all the difference to the Red Sox. Steven Tyler of the rock band Aerosmith boomed out the "Star-Spangled Banner" while F-16 fighter planes from the Vermont Air National Guard soared overhead. The Red Sox struck first, with Ortiz's three-run home run. Red Sox pitcher Tim Wakefield had trouble early and gave up an important home run to Larry Walker. The Red Sox, though, built up a 7-2 lead with important hits by second baseman Mark Bellhorn and catcher Doug Mirabelli. The Cardinals fought back, led by Walker and shortstop Edgar Rentería. A wild throwing error by Red Sox reliever Bronson Arroyo also helped the Cards, and Red Sox fans began to wonder if the curse was alive and well. The score was tied, 7-7, by the seventh inning. Their team had blown a five-run lead!

In the bottom of the seventh, Ortiz hit a line drive so hard that it knocked Cardinals second baseman Tony Womack out of the game when it struck his collarbone. The Sox ended up scoring two runs, and going into the eighth with their closer Keith Foulke, the game seemed safely in hand. It wasn't. The Cards scored two runs in the eighth when Manny Ramírez

Two days before Game 2 of the 2004 World Series, Curt Schilling threw in the bullpen at Fenway Park. Watching him were *(from left)* Red Sox assistant trainer Chris Correnti, team physician William Morgan, head trainer Jim Rowe, and pitching coach Dave Wallace. Even on the morning of Game 2, Schilling was unsure if he would be able to pitch because of his injured ankle.

made two errors on balls hit to left field. The game was tied again. Both teams knew that this first game was crucial, and both were fighting for every pitch and hit.

Some fans would say later that the curse was formally reversed in the last half of the eighth inning. Second baseman Mark Bellhorn, not noted for his power, hit a home run off the right-field foul-pole, just barely fair. The call was disputed but not overturned. Bellhorn became the first second baseman in major-league history to hit home runs in three consecutive postseason games (he had hit ones against the Yankees in Games 6 and 7). He would soon leave the team, unnoticed and unheralded. On this night, though, he was all the difference. The Red Sox won, 11-9. It was the highest-

★ ★ ★ ★ ★

A CURSE REVERSED

Most baseball fans know about The Curse. When Red Sox owner Harry Frazee traded Babe Ruth to the New York Yankees in 1919, the Sox went through a period of misfortune that gave rise to the superstition about "The Curse of the Bambino." (One of Babe Ruth's nicknames was Bambino.) From 1946 to 1986, the Red Sox lost two one-game playoffs (in 1948 and 1978) and four World Series in the seventh and final game of each.

For superstitious fans, each World Series loss by the Sox had a sign of The Curse, and a messenger of The Curse. In the final World Series game in 1946, one of the slowest runners in baseball, St. Louis Cardinal Enos Slaughter, scored the winning run all the way from first base on a single (later ruled a double) when Red Sox shortstop Johnny Pesky strangely hesitated before throwing the relayed baseball to home to try to get Slaughter. It lives in baseball history as "Slaughter's Mad Dash" but some Sox fans know it as "Pesky's Freeze."

In 1967, brilliant Red Sox manager Dick Williams made a rare bad decision and started pitcher Jim Lonborg after only two days' rest in Game 7 of the Series. Lonborg was hit hard, and the St. Louis Cardinals won again. In the final game of the 1975 World Series, Sox pitcher Bill "Spaceman" Lee (later to run for president on the Rhinoceros ticket) threw a very slow trick pitch known as the Eephus pitch (essentially an underhanded throw) to Cincinnati Red Tony Pérez, who hit a game-changing two-

scoring first game of the World Series in history. It was a wild game but not the only one.

Game 2 was also at Fenway Park, and Schilling was the starting pitcher. Fans did not realize that, when Schilling woke

☆ ☆ ☆ ☆ ☆

run home run so hard that the Red Sox outfielders never turned around to watch the ball fly out of the stadium. In 1986, the Sox came within one strike of winning the Series in Game 6, but when a ball rolled through the legs of Red Sox first baseman Bill Buckner, Ray Knight scored the game-winning run and the New York Mets went on to win Game 7 as well.

Gypsy legend has it that blood must be spilled to reverse a curse, and Schilling's sock might have helped. The *Boston Globe* reported a strange incident near the end of the 2004 season that superstitious Sox fans say also qualifies as a curse reverser. Sixteen-year-old Lee Gavin grew up in the same home in Sudbury, Massachusetts, that Babe Ruth lived in while with Boston. Lee was sitting in Fenway Park's right field—Section 9, Box 95, Row AA—on a September 2004 night when a foul ball from the bat of Manny Ramírez struck him in the face, despite the fact that Lee is an excellent fielder and saw the ball coming from 300 feet (91 meters) away. A few drops of his blood fell on the concrete in front of him as he tried to retrieve the ball, and the Red Sox went on an unprecedented winning streak from then on.

More rational fans say that great pitching and good hitting won the 2004 World Series. Still, Chicago Cub and Philadelphia Phillie fans hope they can reverse their own curses without bloodshed.

Faithful Red Sox fans gathered at Fenway Park on October 28, 2004, the day after their team won the World Series. That day, people were seen visiting cemeteries to tell their deceased relatives that The Curse had been broken.

up that morning in his home in Medfield, Massachusetts, he did not think he could pitch that night. His ankle was too damaged and too painful. As he drove toward the field, though, he saw hand-lettered signs that fans had put up around his hometown and along the way to the park. The signs were on telephone poles and fire stations. They were spaced about every mile on the way to Fenway, a long distance. The signs were to Schilling, from his friends and neighbors in Medfield. They wished him luck. They inspired him. He later said that he could not explain it, but he knew he had to pitch that night.

Game 2 was played in a cold mist. The temperatures never got out of the 40s. It was not an ideal night for a pitcher with an injured ankle. Schilling got in trouble right away when Cardinals star Albert Pujols doubled, but when Sox third baseman Bill Mueller snagged a vicious line drive from Scott Rolen, the fans breathed a sigh of relief. The fans could not breathe deeply for long. The Red Sox were soon on their way to making four errors in the game, tying a World Series record. Each time, however, Schilling bore down and made saving pitches. He did not become rattled, as many pitchers do when their fielders let them down. Schilling was the winning pitcher as the Sox held on, 6-2.

Pedro Martínez pitched a great Game 3 at Busch Stadium in St. Louis, retiring the last 14 batters he faced. Derek Lowe won Game 4, the final game, shutting out the Cards, 3-0. When reliever Keith Foulke threw out Edgar Rentería to end the game and the Series, Sox fans all over Boston, New England, and around the country started a celebration heard round the world. A total lunar eclipse was in full progress when the last out was made, and the moon was a blood red that some said was the same color as Schilling's sock.

The next day, an eerie and moving scene played out all over New England. Fans were seen visiting graves of loved ones and placing Red Sox hats, copies of the *Boston Globe,* Sox T-shirts, and other memorabilia on the headstones. New Englanders brought chairs to cemeteries so they could spend the morning or afternoon sharing the glorious victory with someone who was not lucky enough to have seen it. Many souls could now really rest in peace.

The Price
of Glory

Curt Schilling underwent extensive ankle surgery in November 2004 in an attempt to repair the damaged and dislocated tendon once and for all. The operation took three hours, and the repair went beyond the tendon—Schilling also had a bone defect corrected and cartilege restored. He would take many weeks to recover—he spent eight weeks at home in a wheelchair and on crutches. By the time he was able to get out of his wheelchair, spring training was only four weeks away.

The 2004 victory and his role in it were now behind him. He needed to prepare for a new season. He was out of shape and overweight—a natural consequence of being so inactive. When he was later criticized for his condition, he and his family were surprised and astonished at how limited the goodwill of some fans could be. But there was another surprise waiting for him in spring training.

APPEARING IN WASHINGTON

One early March day at the City of Palms Park in Fort Myers, Florida, where he had reported for spring training, a man handed Schilling a piece of paper and asked him to sign it. It was a subpoena, an order to appear in front of the U.S. Congress to discuss steroid use in Major League Baseball. Schilling signed it and returned it to the man, and so became the first player to officially notify Congress that he would appear. He was confused about why he was a part of the hearings. "If there's a guy in the big leagues who is at the bottom of the list as far as being accused of using steroids, I would imagine I'm right in the area." Schilling had publicly criticized steroid use among baseball players, and the congressional panel investigating the issue wanted to hear from him. Schilling also joked to reporters that he would bring a lawyer, in case he said something stupid—which was "a likely possibility."

On March 17, 2005, the country watched the televised congressional hearings, which went on for almost 11 hours. Representative Thomas Davis, the chairman of the House Government Reform Committee, opened the hearings at 10 A.M. and heard from Schilling, former player José Canseco (who had just published a book on steroid use in baseball), retired player Mark McGwire, Orioles first baseman Rafael Palmeiro, Cubs outfielder Sammy Sosa, and others. Schilling spoke early and directed anger at Canseco: He warned Congress against "assisting him [Canseco] to sell more books." Schilling was, as usual, very articulate under fire, saying that more than 90 percent of major-league players do not use steroids and that "the fear of public embarrassment and humiliation upon being caught is going to be greater than any player imagined." He felt that Congress should not intervene in the sport, saying that

Curt Schilling participated in a hearing on steroid use on March 17, 2005, before the House Government Reform Committee in Congress. Also attending were Rafael Palmeiro *(center)* of the Baltimore Orioles and former slugger Mark McGwire *(left)*. Schilling has spoken out strongly against steroids.

Major League Baseball would be better off strengthening and enforcing its own rules to end steroid use. His position would win the day.

Many agree that the biggest loser that day was slugger Mark McGwire, who repeatedly said that "my lawyers have advised me that I cannot answer these questions." When asked if he had taken steroids, he said, "I am not here to talk about the past." He seemed to be admitting to steroid use without wanting to be honest about it. Perhaps the other big loser was Rafael

Palmeiro, who denied using steroids only to be suspended on August 2, 2005, for testing positive for steroids (he said he did not know how that could have happened). He could have been prosecuted for lying under oath to a congressional panel, but the House Government Reform Committee decided not to pursue perjury charges against Palmeiro.

Some have said that Schilling reminds them of Hall of Fame pitcher Jim Bunning, who was a famous fastballer in the 1950s and 1960s. Bunning went on to become a U.S. representative from Kentucky, and he was on the House committee that led the hearing on steroid use. Bunning said, "When I played with Henry Aaron, Willie Mays, and Ted Williams, they didn't put on 40 pounds . . . and they didn't hit more home runs in their late thirties as they did in their late twenties. What's happening in baseball is not natural, and it's not right."

2005: AN INJURY-PLAGUED YEAR

The Yankees saw the success that Schilling brought to the Red Sox in 2004, and they decided to try to bring some pitching magic to their team in 2005. They traded for Randy Johnson, who would never feel as comfortable in New York as Schilling felt in Boston. Johnson had won five Cy Young Awards and was the oldest pitcher ever to throw a perfect game (giving up no runs, no hits, and no walks in a complete nine-inning game). The Yankees had not won a World Series since 2000, and their owner and fans were impatient. Johnson would be their Schilling. Yankee manager Joe Torre said, "Schilling was the big difference last year. Schilling and Ortiz just beat us up, and I'm not trying to downplay anyone else." The baseball world could not wait for an Opening Day showdown between the former teammates who now played for bitter rivals.

The much anticipated Johnson-Schilling pitching matchup on Opening Day in New York did not happen because Schilling's ankle had not healed quickly enough. The Red Sox did receive their 2004 World Championship rings that day, however. Considered one of the ultimate sports collectibles, the ring has 1.89 carats of small diamonds in a circle around more than 2 carats of rubies making a "B." The ring says "Greatest Comeback in History" and "8 Straight Wins." When one was put on eBay for sale, the bidding was above $100,000 (author Stephen King was interested in purchasing it).

Schilling came back to pitching in mid-April, but in just three games that month, his ERA was 8.15 and he lost two games and won only one. He went on the disabled list and began to get the full rehabilitation work he had skipped by trying too hard to get ready for Opening Day.

When he returned from rehabilitating in Arizona later in the spring, he had to simply watch his teammates from a distance. He still was not able to play. "He looked like a kid who has chicken pox and has to sit at the window and watch everybody playing outside," Shonda Schilling said. Finally, beginning in July, he was used as a reliever to get in some work. He returned to the starting rotation on September 5. He soon beat the Yankees but then lost to the Oakland A's. A typical game was the one against the A's on September 15, 2005. The Red Sox were in first place in the American League East, but barely. They were losing ground to the dreaded Yankees. On this night, they needed to win because they could see from the out-of-town scoreboard that the Yankees were beating the Tampa Bay Devil Rays, 9-5. After five pitches by Schilling, the Red Sox were down 2-0. Mark Kotsay of the A's knocked in two batters on the fifth pitch of game. Schilling was shaky for the first three innings before finally getting in his groove. But it was too late. "I left a lot of balls over the middle of the plate," Schilling told reporters. Manager Terry Francona said, "Hitters let you know. I think it's more location than zip on his fastball."

Schilling's ERA for the season rose to the worst he has ever had—5.69. That meant his team had to score six runs a game on average to win when he was pitching. His record

After giving up an RBI single, Curt Schilling yelled in frustration during a game against the Oakland Athletics on September 15, 2005. Schilling's injured ankle took a long time to rehabilitate, and Schilling ended up having a dismal season in 2005, with an ERA of 5.69 and a record of 8–8.

was 8–8. The team was disappointing its fans, and yet most people knew how much Schilling had done only a year before and accepted his off year. In fact, they still cheered Schilling whenever they could. That led to some bitter feelings among a few teammates, who felt that Schilling should have been booed as much as they were. One unnamed player said so to reporters. That hurt Schilling, a man of deep emotions. "Purely on a professional level, this year has been by far the hardest for me of my career," he told *Boston Globe* reporter Bob Hohler on September 27.

Shonda told the same reporter, "My heart is hurting because he's not the same person and I don't know how to help him. I don't ever remember feeling as happy for him as I feel badly for him now. It's a horrible feeling." Schilling summarized his year just before the postseason: "I'm trying as hard as I can to get back and be part of this thing this year. But, God willing, if we get into the postseason and do well and win again, it will still never be like last year. Nothing will be like last year." At the end of the regular season, *Boston Globe* writer Jackie MacMullan summed up Schilling's year.

> You want him to be something he can't be right now. Curt Schilling was a god out of Greek mythology last season. He was Paul Bunyan, bigger than life, an indestructible action hero with the flesh wounds—and the bloody sock—to prove it. His heroics came at a price, and the burly righthander—as well as the Red Sox—are paying for it now. . . . At present, Schilling is a mere mortal trying to find his way through the most vexing season of his 15-year career.

The 2005 season ended when the Red Sox were bumped from first place by the Yankees and then swept by the Chicago White Sox in the American League Division Series. The fact that the White Sox went on to win the World Series was little comfort. Like many teams, the Red Sox had lost too many players to hang onto their championship. Pedro Martínez was gone. So were Derek Lowe, Mark Bellhorn, and many others. Johnny Damon left after the 2005 season. But Schilling and David Ortiz would be coming back with many other talented players for the 2006 season, and fans looked forward to it.

2006 AND BEYOND

At the start of spring training in 2006 in Fort Myers, Schilling told reporters, "I'm ready to be good again." He was healthy, in shape, and wearing off-color T-shirts that offended some and made others laugh. One reporter suggested that he should wear a T-shirt that said, "I'm Back . . . and Somebody's Going to Pay." Schilling was usually in a good mood, especially during spring training, when he could enjoy his teammates without the pressure of winning. One of his new teammates was Josh Beckett, a young pitcher traded from the Florida Marlins and one of the best young arms in baseball. Schilling knew that he needed to be part of a one-two punch to be effective, and now he had that again—at least temporarily.

The 2006 season started well for the Red Sox, and Schilling, Beckett, and David Ortiz helped them to a spot in first place. Then the season fell apart—Beckett had control problems and was injured, Jason Varitek (the catcher and team captain) hurt his knee, and injuries to other key players started to escalate. Ortiz went on to set a single-season record for home runs by a Red Sox player (54), and Schilling pitched well, with a 15–7 record and an ERA under 4.00, but that was not enough to carry the team. After Manny Ramírez became injured and did not play much at the end of the season, the team finished in third place in the American League East and out of the play-offs.

The season did have some highlights for Schilling. On May 27, he earned his 200th career victory, a key milestone for any pitcher hoping to get into the Baseball Hall of Fame. On July 9, he made his 400th career start, against the Chicago White

Sox at U.S. Cellular Field. And on August 30, he recorded his 3,000th strikeout, against Nick Swisher of the Oakland A's. He was only the third pitcher in major-league history to reach that milestone before reaching the 1,000-career-walks mark. The other two are Ferguson Jenkins and Greg Maddux.

During the winter before the 2007 season, the Red Sox obtained the rights to Japanese pitching sensation Daisuke

★ ★ ★ ★ ★

HOW FAST IS FAST?

Pitching a baseball so that it travels 100 miles per hour (161 kilometers per hour) is something very few people have been able to do. Walter Johnson could throw a baseball 100 miles per hour, almost certainly. So could Bob Feller, Sandy Koufax, Nolan Ryan, Randy Johnson, and Curt Schilling. So can a few others. One problem is that only in the past few decades have people been able to measure the speed of a pitched ball accurately.

The radar gun came into existence in the 1950s and into common use in baseball when Curt Schilling was in grade school. A radar gun is a device that transmits and receives radio signals (much like an automatic garage door opener or a keyless car lock), measuring the speed of the object it is aimed at by calculating the difference between the radio waves sent and received.

The *Guinness Book of World Records* notes the fastest pitch ever—100.9 miles per hour, thrown by Nolan Ryan in 1974. Some argue that Mark Wohlers threw a pitch at 103 miles per hour as recorded by a radar gun in spring training in 1995 and published in the *Baseball Almanac*. Oldtimers say that at an exhibition Bob Feller threw a baseball faster than a motorcycle traveling 104 mph.

To throw 100 miles per hour, a pitcher has to have several things happen in precise order. A pitcher needs to rock back onto his back leg, and then thrust forward while rotating his pelvis

Matsuzaka (known as Dice-K). The team was counting on having Schilling and Beckett remain healthy and getting a third pitcher who could also win at least 15 games. The Red Sox had to pay more than $100 million for Dice-K, gambling that he could be a winner in the American League and that he would not upset the team chemistry and turn it into a witch's brew. Some players can be very resentful when other players make so

and trunk just before whipping his elbow, shoulder, and wrist in exactly the right sequence. Human tendons, muscles, and ligaments have a breaking point that does not allow them to twist and push faster than a certain amount. That upper limit of force seems to be right around the level that goes into throwing a baseball 100 miles per hour.

Baseball legend has it that the fastest pitcher of them all was Steve Dalkowski. The 5-foot-11-inch, 170-pound (180-centimeter, 77-kilogram) lefty never made it to the big leagues. For one thing, he was too wild. A very early version of the radar gun could not pick up the speed of his pitches because it could not locate them. He reportedly threw at 105 miles per hour (169 kilometers per hour) or more. He once threw a baseball over a fence 440 feet (134 meters) away. Another time, he broke an umpire's face mask in three places, knocking the umpire back some 18 feet (5.5 meters). Legend has it that, after he hit a batter in the ear, tearing away a piece of it, he became even wilder. He was due to make his first major-league start in 1963 when he fielded a bunt in an exhibition game and somehow blew out his arm throwing to first base. The character played by Brendan Fraser in the movie *The Scout* is loosely based on Dalkowski, as is the character played by Tim Robbins in the movie *Bull Durham* (named Nick Laloosh in the movie).

Curt Schilling acknowledged the crowd's applause in Oakland after he recorded the 3,000th strikeout of his career against Nick Swisher in a game on August 30, 2006. Schilling had a much better year in 2006 than in 2005, but the Red Sox finished in third place in the American League East.

much money. As it turned out, the gamble was not a bad one: Dice-K won exactly 15 games in the 2007 regular season, while losing 12, and he did not become a distraction. He was even picked over Schilling to start Game 2 of the 2007 American League Division Series, a sign that Dice-K had fit into the starting rotation nicely.

Schilling by 2007 was clearly an aging pitcher. Very few pitchers can be effective beyond 40 years of age, but Roger Clemens has proven that, with superb training, the ravages of time can be held at bay for at least a few years. Schilling will use his head and his heart and make the best of what he has left. The 2007 spring training gossip was about his new changeup, since his fastest fastball is slowing down. He will be boisterous as well as a team leader. He cannot change now.

Schilling's 2007 season did not start well. On Opening Day, April 2, he was hit hard by the Kansas City Royals, and the Red Sox lost 7-1. By early June, though, he had pitched his way back to greatness, missing a no-hitter by only one out on June 7. That day he threw the third one-hitter of his career, and his first complete-game shutout in more than four years. He looked as good as ever.

But the one-hitter was to be the high point of his 2007 regular season. A starting pitcher's health is always in jeopardy, especially at Schilling's age. Throwing a baseball so hard for so long is just not a natural act. He was diagnosed with shoulder tendonitis in mid-June and missed almost two months. When he returned to the team in August, he lost more games than he won. His split-finger fastball seemed to abandon him at times. He could no longer throw 95-mile-per-hour (153-kilometer-per-hour) fastballs, so he could rarely fool batters with change-ups. He made mistakes more often than he had in the past.

On September 16, he started a crucial game against the Yankees, facing former mentor and current archrival Roger Clemens in a classic matchup recalling the famous Game 7 of the 2001 World Series. Schilling lasted longer than Clemens, but when Yankee Derek Jeter slammed an 84-mph (135-kph) Schilling splitter out of Fenway Park for a three-run home run, the Red Sox were stunned enough to lose that game and the next three, losing much of their lead in the American League East.

The Red Sox, however, were able to hold off the Yankees to win their division and make the play-offs. In the American League Division Series against the Angels, the Sox won the first two games at home. Schilling had the start in Game 3, and he pitched seven scoreless innings as Boston won the game, 9-1, to sweep the series.

In the next round, the Red Sox won the first game against the Cleveland Indians but lost the next three. Boston took Game 5 in Cleveland, and still facing elimination, headed back to Fenway Park. Schilling started Game 6 and gave up only two runs in seven innings as the Red Sox cruised to a 12-2 victory. Boston's bats continued to be hot in Game 7, with the Red Sox winning 11-2 to complete another stellar comeback in a championship series.

In the World Series, Boston faced the Colorado Rockies, who had won 21 of their previous 22 games. The Rockies, though, hit a wall against the Sox. For the second time in four years, the Red Sox swept their opponents in the World Series. Schilling was the winner of Game 2, a 2-1 nail-biter at Fenway. With the victory, Schilling became the only pitcher to win World Series games in his 20s, 30s, and 40s.

"I'm definitely more nervous now at this stage in my career," Schilling said after Game 2. "I think it's because I know things are winding down and now I look around and enjoy so many things around me. . . . When I was young, it was just getting myself ready 24/7. Now I'm enjoying what I'm getting to see."

Eventually Schilling will leave Boston and the major leagues. When he does, he will leave behind a legacy of world championships and a competitive spirit that will be remembered for as long as the game is played. But he is a man of many talents, and he just might make a bigger mark on the world when he leaves baseball.

Faith, Family, and Business

There was one other aspect of the famous Game 6 in the 2004 American League Championship Series against the Yankees, the bloody-sock game, that Curt Schilling has talked about but few have mentioned. He had talked to his pastor hours before the game about what to pray for. He resolved not to pray for victory that night, but he did pray for strength. Schilling had become a devout Christian in 1997 and had woven his strong faith into every aspect of his life. After Game 6, he told reporters, "I've never been touched by God as I was tonight. . . . I tried to go out and do it myself in Game 1, and you saw what happened. Tonight was God's work on the mound." Athletes invoking God make many people uncomfortable—surely there are devoutly religious souls on both sides of any competition. Schilling, however, is

Curt Schilling autographed a Harley Davidson motorcycle in September 2004 at Fenway Park in Boston. The motorcycle was auctioned off to raise money in support of amyotrophic lateral sclerosis (ALS) and melanoma research and patient care. The Schillings are involved in many causes and helped to house a family from New Orleans after Hurricane Katrina in 2005.

outspoken about everything in his life, and he unashamedly proclaims his religious faith. "I've learned you should never hide your faith."

A FAMILY FROM NEW ORLEANS

The Schillings were as moved as most Americans by what they saw of the toll taken in 2005 by Hurricane Katrina in New Orleans. They decided to help, as they usually do. "When we realized how many people had nowhere to go, we didn't just want to make a donation," Shonda Schilling said. "We all need to take care of each other at a time like this." They arranged to have a large family flown to the Boston area and put up in a hotel. The Fields family had seven children, four boys and three girls. They had fled the storm with only some clothes. They had never been to the Northeast and had no idea who these anonymous benefactors offering them help were, but they accepted the offer to come north. They had nowhere else to go.

The Fields flew to Boston and checked into a hotel. When the Schilling family visited them, Efrem Fields finally knew who these helpers were. "Wait a second, I know this guy," said Fields, a baseball fan. "It blew my mind," he said. "They are beautiful people, God-loving people."

The four Schilling children and the seven Fields children instantly became friends and played together often. The Schilling kids brought them toys and games. Shonda watched the two sets of young people interact. "I'm trying not to cry when I see them. . . . It's a beautiful family, and they are all together."

The Schillings did not want the publicity that the story stirred up, but the publicity helped the Fields family. The town of Hudson, Massachusetts, offered for them to live in a house owned by the South Middlesex Opportunity Council, a nonprofit organization. Efrem and his wife, Shelita, got jobs. Their children enrolled in the Hudson schools. Twelve-year-old Efrem, Jr., said, "People are cool here. They don't do the stuff that they do where I'm from." Emaj, one of the children, loved the change of seasons. She said, "I thought it was cool to see the snow. It was my first time. I cried. All you see is white."

Fields said that one of his daughters made her first snow angel. He told her it would be easier if she did not make it with her face down in the snow.

GOING INTO BUSINESS

Ever since Schilling had played "Wizardry" on his Apple II, he has been hooked on video games. In October 2006, he took that interest and turned it into a business. He started Green Monster Games, a company that would specialize in online video gaming, a dramatically growing segment of the industry. He personally interviewed and hired every employee, and as the CEO/president and founder he could

☆ ☆ ☆ ☆ ☆

THE MEDFIELD FACTOR

The people of Medfield, Massachusetts (a town southwest of Boston), are used to seeing some combination of Gehrig, Gabriella, Grant, and Garrison Schilling walking down Main Street with one or both of their parents. They shop at CVS or Lord's Department Store. Schilling can be found dropping one of the kids off at preschool or one of the Medfield schools. Medfield residents know that the Schillings bought the house that former New England Patriots quarterback Drew Bledsoe had lived in. The house, on 26 acres off of Woodbridge Road, cost the Schillings more than $4 million.

Shonda Schilling can be seen at Graceful Stitches on Main Street, an organization whose volunteers knit clothing items. All proceeds from the items are donated to cancer-related charities. Shonda ordered 50 red and blue knitted scarves from Graceful Stitches and gave them to the Red Sox players' wives. They were good luck.

control most aspects of the business, even though he had little formal business training. He had negotiated his own contracts with various major-league teams, so he had some hands-on experience with business issues and an instinctive knack for business deals. But video-game development and servicing was a very costly enterprise, and Schilling had to search for investors.

Green Monster Games hired some very talented people, including Todd McFarlane, the creator of the *Spawn* comic book series. GMG's creative director was R.A. Salvatore, a noted science fiction author. By March 2007, though, GMG had a name change, to 38 Studios. Schilling's uniform

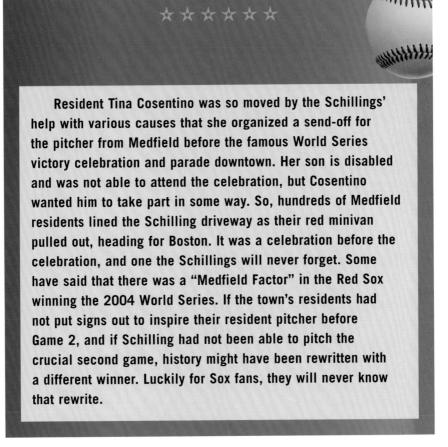

★ ★ ★ ★ ★ ★

Resident Tina Cosentino was so moved by the Schillings' help with various causes that she organized a send-off for the pitcher from Medfield before the famous World Series victory celebration and parade downtown. Her son is disabled and was not able to attend the celebration, but Cosentino wanted him to take part in some way. So, hundreds of Medfield residents lined the Schilling driveway as their red minivan pulled out, heading for Boston. It was a celebration before the celebration, and one the Schillings will never forget. Some have said that there was a "Medfield Factor" in the Red Sox winning the 2004 World Series. If the town's residents had not put signs out to inspire their resident pitcher before Game 2, and if Schilling had not been able to pitch the crucial second game, history might have been rewritten with a different winner. Luckily for Sox fans, they will never know that rewrite.

Curt Schilling tried to slay the dragon Hurricannus while enjoying the online video game *EverQuest II* in April 2005 at the Sony Online Entertainment Fan Faire in Atlanta. Schilling has started his own online gaming company, now known as 38 Studios—his uniform number is 38.

number had been 38 wherever he pitched, and the name change was important. The Red Sox had declined to extend Schilling's contract in the spring of 2007, making him a free agent at the end of 2007. "Green Monster" is the name of the famous 37-foot-high (11-meter-high) green left-field wall in Boston's Fenway Park, and changing the name of his company made Schilling more independent of the Red Sox.

38 Studios would focus on multiplayer online role-playing games, an established and growing market. Salvatore told a business reporter that these sites varied from "glorified chatrooms to cooperative adventure." Schilling's company wanted to develop games that were more adventures than chatrooms. The creative director went on to say, "Ten years from now, more people will be playing computer games than are watching television." Schilling's confident spirit infected the whole company.

A MAN OF MANY INTERESTS

Schilling had been collecting war memorabilia for many years, especially that of World War II. He would eventually amass more than 2,000 books on the subject. He owns a small demolition vehicle that the German army used to clear mine-fields in World War II. He also has many helmets and knives used in the war. One of his prize possessions is a brown beret that British Field Marshal Bernard Montgomery wore during the African campaign in the war. "Monty's" victory at El Alamein in North Africa in 1942 was a turning point in the war. Montgomery was a larger-than-life character, noted for his intense preparation, controversial views on almost everything, and for famously saying he was "too busy" to attend his mother's funeral.

Schilling also collects baseball memorabilia and has a Lou Gehrig jersey and a Roberto Clemente bat. He is an avid fan of the Pittsburgh Steelers and must have been delighted in their February 2006 Super Bowl victory. He is famous for his T-shirts, both wearing them and inspiring them. Legend has it that a T-shirt that sold well in Boston, with "Killin' With Schillin'" on the front and "Yankee Hater—.38" on the back, had to be pulled from circulation because the city's murder rate started to go up.

Curt Schilling introduced President George W. Bush during a re-election campaign rally on November 1, 2004, in Wilmington, Ohio. Some people believe that Schilling may himself run for public office one day.

Schilling showed how varied his interests are when he went on a celebrity version of the popular TV game show *Jeopardy!* On November 9, 2006, he donated his $25,000 winnings to charity.

His favorite game is *Advanced Squad Leader* (known as *ASL*). The game is constantly with him on road trips, and he even started a magazine entitled *ASL Journal* that is devoted to the game. He also likes to play *EverQuest II* and has reviewed the game's expansion packs for *PC Gamer* magazine. The creators of the game made Schilling a special online character, and in 2006 fans were able to battle the virtual Schilling. Every time he was defeated, Sony Online Entertainment donated money toward ALS research.

A POLITICAL ANIMAL

Schilling's political views became controversial in 2004. He campaigned for President George W. Bush's re-election after the 2004 World Series victory, even though the Red Sox management and ownership were campaigning for Massachusetts Senator John Kerry, the Democratic candidate. He has been encouraged to run for Kerry's Senate seat in 2008, as a Republican. He has refused to say much about that possibility.

On January 29, 2007, Schilling announced that he would support Senator John McCain of Arizona in the 2008 presidential election. He criticized Senator Hillary Clinton for her comments on the war in Iraq. He has remained supportive of President Bush, although he disagrees with him more than he had in the past.

Many people who know Schilling believe he will seriously consider running for political office. He is opinionated, a man of deep convictions and faith, and he wants to be heard. He wants to make a difference. Whether he pitches or runs for office in 2008, he will do it with all his heart and soul. He does not know any other way. He never has.

STATISTICS

CURT SCHILLING
Primary position: Pticher

Full Name: Curtis Montague Schilling
Born: November 14, 1966, Anchorage,
Alaska • Height: 6'4" Weight: 230 lbs.
Teams: Baltimore Orioles (1988–1990);
Houston Astros (1991); Philadelphia Phillies
(1992–2000); Arizona Diamondbacks (2000–
2003); Boston Red Sox (2004–present)

✫ ✫ ✫ ✫ ✫ ✫

YEAR	TEAM	G	W–L	ERA	SO	BB
1988	BAL	4	0–3	9.82	4	10
1989	BAL	5	0–1	6.23	6	3
1990	BAL	35	1–2	2.54	32	19
1991	HOU	56	3–5	3.81	71	39
1992	PHI	42	14–11	2.35	147	59
1993	PHI	34	16–7	4.02	186	57
1994	PHI	13	2–8	4.48	58	28
1995	PHI	17	7–5	3.57	114	26
1996	PHI	26	9–10	3.19	182	50
1997	PHI	35	17–11	2.97	319	58
1998	PHI	35	15–14	3.25	300	61
1999	PHI	24	15–6	3.54	152	44
2000	PHI/ARI	29	11–12	3.81	168	45
2001	ARI	35	22–6	2.98	293	39
2002	ARI	36	23–7	3.23	316	33
2003	ARI	24	8–9	2.95	194	32

Key: BAL = Baltimore Orioles; HOU = Houston Astros; PHI = Philadelphia Phillies;
ARI = Arizona Diamondbacks; BOS = Boston Red Sox; G = Games; W = Wins;
L = Losses; ERA = Earned run average; SO = Strikeouts: BB = Bases on balls

☆ ☆ ☆ ☆ ☆

YEAR	TEAM	G	W-L	ERA	SO	BB
2004	BOS	32	21–6	3.26	203	53
2005	BOS	32	8–8	5.69	87	22
2006	BOS	31	15–7	3.97	183	28
2007	BOS	24	9–8	3.87	101	23
TOTALS		569	216–146	3.46	3,116	711

Key: BAL = Baltimore Orioles; HOU = Houston Astros; PHI = Philadelphia Phillies; ARI = Arizona Diamondbacks; BOS = Boston Red Sox; G = Games; W = Wins; L = Losses; ERA = Earned run average; SO = Strikeouts: BB = Bases on balls

CHRONOLOGY

1966   **November 14**   Born Curtis Montague Schilling in Anchorage, Alaska.

1986   **January 14**   Drafted in the second round by the Boston Red Sox.

Played in the Junior College World Series for Yavapai Junior College.

May 30   Signed contract with the Red Sox.

1988   **January**   His father, Cliff Schilling, dies.

July 29   Traded to the Baltimore Orioles.

September 7   Makes pitching debut in the major leagues against the Red Sox.

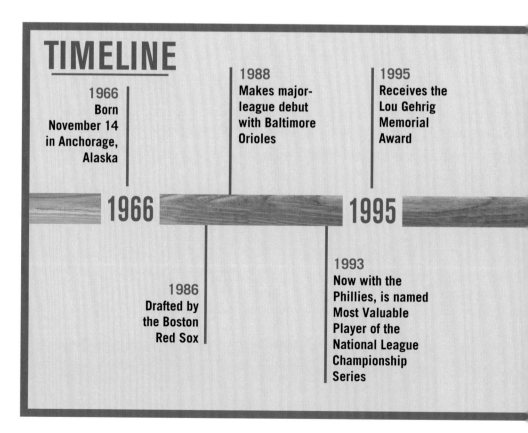

TIMELINE

1966
Born
November 14
in Anchorage,
Alaska

1988
Makes major-
league debut
with Baltimore
Orioles

1995
Receives the
Lou Gehrig
Memorial
Award

1966   **1995**

1986
Drafted by
the Boston
Red Sox

1993
Now with the
Phillies, is named
Most Valuable
Player of the
National League
Championship
Series

1990   Meets Shonda Brewer, his future wife.

1991   **January 10** Traded to the Houston Astros.

1992   Chewed out by Roger Clemens for wasting his talent as a pitcher; marries Shonda Brewer.

        April 2 Traded to the Philadelphia Phillies.

1993   Named Most Valuable Player of the National League Championship Series; Phillies lose World Series to the Toronto Blue Jays.

1994   **August 12** Major League Baseball players go on strike; walkout lasts until April 1995.

1995   Receives the Lou Gehrig Memorial Award.

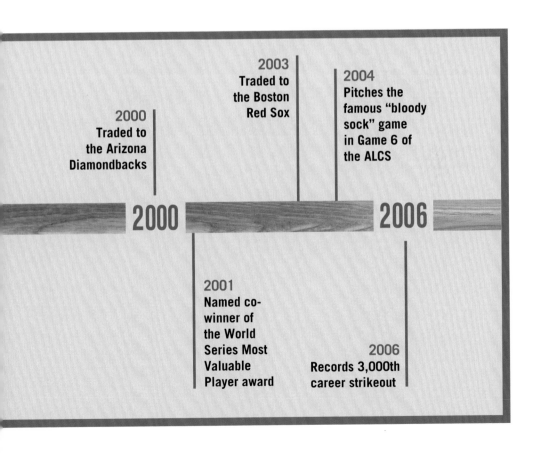

2000
Traded to the Arizona Diamondbacks

2003
Traded to the Boston Red Sox

2004
Pitches the famous "bloody sock" game in Game 6 of the ALCS

2000

2006

2001
Named co-winner of the World Series Most Valuable Player award

2006
Records 3,000th career strikeout

2000   **July 26** Traded to the Arizona Diamondbacks.

2001   Named co-winner of the Most Valuable Player award for the World Series, along with Diamondbacks teammate Randy Johnson; goes 4–0 in the postseason with a 1.12 ERA; Diamondbacks defeat the Yankees in a thrilling seven-game series to win the World Series.

2003   **November 29** Traded to the Boston Red Sox.

2004   **October 19** Pitches the famous "bloody sock" game in Game 6 of the American League Championship Series against the New York Yankees.

Red Sox sweep the St. Louis Cardinals to win their first World Series in 86 years. Has surgery on his ankle after the Series.

2005   **March 17** Appears before Congress to testify about steroid use in professional baseball.

2006   **May 27:** Gets 200th career victory.

July 9 Makes 400th career start.

August 30 Records 3,000th career strikeout.

GLOSSARY

at-bat　An official turn at batting that is charged to a baseball player, except when the player walks, sacrifices, is hit by a pitched ball, or is interfered with by a catcher. At-bats are used to calculate a player's batting average and slugging percentage.

ball　When a pitched ball is not in the strike zone, the home-plate umpire calls it a ball, provided the batter has not swung.

base on balls　When a batter receives four pitches out of the strike zone, the batter receives a base on balls, also called a walk, and goes to first base.

batter's box　The area to the left and right of home plate where a batter must stand during his or her time at bat.

bullpen　The area where pitchers warm up, usually behind the outfield fences. The name comes from its similarity to where bulls are kept before a bullfight.

catcher　The defensive player directly behind home plate, whose job is to signal to the pitcher which kind of pitch to throw and where to throw it. This player also catches the pitch. Good catchers know hitters' strengths and weaknesses and can "frame" their catches to influence umpires to call more strikes.

changeup　A slow pitch thrown with the same motion as a fastball in order to deceive the batter.

curveball　A pitch thrown so that it spins in such a way that the ball curves to the left, right, or downward from a straight path to the strike zone.

double　When a batter reaches second base safely on a hit, he or she has hit a double.

doubleheader　Two baseball games played by the same teams on the same day.

dugout   The area where the players and coaches not on the field can wait and watch. It usually has a bench with a roof, and in the major leagues includes a bat rack, glove and towel holders, a water cooler, a telephone to the bullpen, and more.

earned run average (ERA)   The average number of runs a pitcher allows per nine-inning game; the runs must be scored without errors by defensive players.

error   When a defensive player makes a mistake resulting in a runner reaching base or advancing a base, an error is designated by the game's scorer.

fastball   A pitch that is thrown so that it has maximum speed. It can be gripped in any number of ways, most commonly touching two baseball seams (a two-seamer) with the index finger and middle finger, or across four seams (a four-seamer).

full count   If a batter has three balls and two strikes, he or she has a full count.

grand slam   A home run with three runners on base, resulting in four runs for the offensive team. The grand slam is one of the most dramatic plays in baseball.

home run   When a batter hits a ball into the stands in fair territory, it is a home run. The batter may also get an inside-the-park home run if the ball never leaves the playing field and the runner is able to reach home plate without stopping before being tagged by a defensive player. A home run counts as one run, and if there are any runners on base when a home run is hit, they too score.

inning   The time during which each team has come to bat and each has made three outs. The top of an inning is when the visiting team bats, and bottom of an inning is when the home team bats. So, each inning has two half-innings. In

Major League Baseball, a standard game is nine innings. In college baseball, it may be seven or nine. In Little League, it may be three to six innings.

knuckleball   A slow pitch that is thrown with little spin by gripping the ball with the knuckles or the tips of the fingers. The pitch moves erratically and unpredictably.

line drive   A batted ball, usually hit hard, that never gets too far off the ground. Typically a line drive will get beyond the infield without touching the ground or will be hit directly at a player and be caught before it touches the ground.

on deck   The offensive player next in line to bat after the current batter is said to be on deck. Often the player on deck will swing a weighted bat to warm up and stay in an area called the on-deck circle.

perfect game   A special no-hitter in which each batter is retired consecutively, allowing no base runners through walks, errors, or any other means.

relief pitcher   A pitcher brought in to substitute for (or "relieve") another pitcher.

save   A statistic credited to a pitcher who comes into the game with his team leading and completes the game without giving up the lead. The pitcher must be the last pitcher in the game and must fulfill at least one of the following conditions: He comes into the game with a lead of no more than three runs and pitches at least one full inning; he comes into the game with the potential tying or winning run on base, at bat, or on deck; he pitches effectively for at least three innings after entering the game.

single   A batted ball resulting in a hitter reaching first base without a defensive player making an error.

slider   A pitch that is a combination of fastball and curveball—curving near the end of its flight.

splitter   A fastball thrown with the ball gripped as for a forkball. The ball drops rapidly as it nears the plate. It is also known as a split-fingered fastball or a split-finger.

strike   A pitch in the strike zone not swung at by the batter, a pitch swung at and missed by the batter, a ball batted foul with less than two strikes, a bunt batted foul with two strikes, or a ball swung at and barely hit that continues into the catcher's glove and is caught. A batter is allowed two strikes and is out on a third strike.

strikeout   When a batter either swings and misses at a third strike or takes a pitch called a third strike, he or she has struck out. A batter can also strike out by bunting foul with two strikes or by hitting a foul tip into the catcher's glove.

strike zone   The area directly over home plate up to the batter's chest (roughly where the uniform lettering is) and down to his or her knees. Different umpires have slightly different strike zones, and players only ask that they be consistent.

tag   The act of a defensive player touching a runner with his glove or hand while the defensive player is in possession of the ball. The runner is out when tagged.

triple   When a batter safely reaches third base on a hit, he or she has hit a triple.

umpire   The official who rules on plays. For most baseball games, a home-plate umpire calls ball and strikes, and other umpires in the infield rule on outs at bases.

walk   A base on balls.

walk-off home run   A game-ending home run by the home team—so named because the losing team has to walk off the field.

windup   A series of regular and distinctive motions made by a pitcher before releasing a pitch.

World Series   A championship series, usually the best four-out-of-seven games. In Major League Baseball, the World Series comes after teams have been through a League Division Series (a best three-out-of-five series) and a League Championship Series (a best four-out-of-seven series).

BIBLIOGRAPHY

Adair, Robert K. *The Physics of Baseball.* 3rd ed. New York: HarperCollins, 2002.

Brown, Matthew L. "Schilling's Virtual Curve Ball." *Worcester Business Journal,* March 19, 2007.

Chass, Murray. "The Complete and Candid Schilling." *New York Times,* May 23, 1999.

Curry, Jack. "Schilling Is the First to Say He Will Testify." *New York Times,* March 12, 2005.

Hohler, Bob. "Painful Season Eats at Schilling." *Boston Globe,* September 27, 2005.

Lewis, Michael. *Moneyball: The Art of Winning an Unfair Game.* New York: W. W. Norton & Company, 2003.

MacMullan, Jackie. "Mortality Replaces Miracles." *Boston Globe.* September 28, 2005.

Olasky, Marvin. "Curt Schilling." *World Magazine,* March 19, 2005.

Rosenthal, Ken. "Heat and Heart: On the Field, in the Community and at Ground Zero, Curt Schilling Made a Difference in 2001." *Sporting News,* December 17, 2001.

Rosinski, Jennifer. "Still Picking Up the Pieces: At Home in a Town's Embrace." *Boston Globe,* August 20, 2006.

Schworm, Peter. "Schilling Family Is Hosting Nine from New Orleans." *Boston Globe,* September 6, 2005.

Stickgold, Emma. "Local Twist on Red Sox Pride: Neighbors Overjoyed by Schilling's Performance." *Boston Globe,* November 4, 2004.

Stout, Glenn. *On the Mound with Curt Schilling.* New York: Matt Christopher, Little Brown & Company, 2004.

FURTHER READING

Aoki, Naomi. "On, Off the Mound, Schilling Makes His Pitch." *Boston Globe,* June 13, 2004.

Golenbock, Peter. *Red Sox Nation: An Unexpurgated History of the Boston Red Sox.* Chicago: Triumph Books, 2005.

Hermoso, Rafael. "Baseball: Wheeling and Dealing, Epstein Got His Man." *New York Times,* November 30, 2003.

Kisseloff, Jeff. *Who Is Baseball's Greatest Hitter?* New York: Henry Holt, 2000.

Nowlin, Bill, and Jim Price. *Blood Feud: The Red Sox, the Yankees, and the Struggle of Good Versus Evil.* Burlington, Mass.: Rounder Books, 2005.

Page, Bob. *Tales from the Diamondbacks Dugout.* Champaign, Ill.: Sports Publishing, 2002.

Shaughnessy, Dan. *Reversing the Curse.* Boston: Houghton Mifflin Co., 2005.

Vecsey, George. "Arizona Makes Some New History." *New York Times,* November 5, 2001.

WEB SITES

38 Pitches: Curt Schilling's Official Blog
http://38pitches.com/

38 Studios
http://www.38studios.com/

The ALS Association
http://www.alsa.org/

Baseball Almanac
http://www.baseball-almanac.com

Baseball Reference
http://www.baseball-reference.com

Curt's Pitch for ALS

http://www.curtspitchforals.org

The Official Site of the Boston Red Sox

http:// boston.redsox.mlb.com

The Official Site of Major League Baseball

http://mlb.mlb.com

The Shade Foundation: The Curt and Shonda Schilling Melanoma Foundation

http://www.shadefoundation.org/

PICTURE CREDITS

INDEX

ABOUT THE AUTHOR

CLIFFORD W. MILLS is a writer and editor living in Jacksonville, Florida. He has written biographies of Derek Jeter, Bernie Williams, Pope Benedict XVI, and Virginia Woolf, compiled a volume of essays about J.D. Salinger, and has been an editor for John Wiley and Sons and Oxford University Press. He played baseball in college and had dreams of pitching for the Red Sox.